MURDER
at Tri-City Mall

MURDER
at Tri-City Mall

BY: BERNIE ZIEGNER

ISBN: 979-8-89021-421-8 Paperback
ISBN: 979-8-89021-422-5 Hardback
ISBN: 979-8-89021-420-1 eBook

Printed in the United States of America.

MURDER AT TRI-CITY MALL

Dino had to get the briefcase away from the man before he reached the bank—he had to. A muffled shot, made in desperation, didn't seem to attract attention in the noisy mall. However, Jennifer witnessed the botched robbery from across the mall as the man collapsed. Dino picked up the briefcase as panic overwhelmed him—he had been observed. He rushed to intercept the witness as she ran toward the main mall exit.

Tim and his reporter friend, Greg, helped Jennifer elude those who wanted her silenced, if not to disappear altogether. The contents of the briefcase would disclose the depth and breadth of the mob investment and money-laundering scheme, and would set the stage for violence and murder.

CHAPTER 1

Dino had been unlucky. He should have been right up to the guy when the man got out of his car. But he hadn't been able to keep up with him in the noon traffic. His target was now but a dozen yards from the mall doorway just as Dino parked. He feared to fail and have the wrath of Angelo to deal with. He wiped at the sweat on his brow. Angelo had told him when the man would be leaving his job and what he looked like and that Dino had to get the man's briefcase or satchel or whatever he was carrying before the man entered the bank. He didn't know what was so important about the briefcase, just told to be sure to grab it. He now rushed to catch up to the man before the guy got to the bank. He *had* to get the briefcase. He put his hand to his sweaty upper lip making sure the mustache was well attached as he ran to the mall doorway, a minor alcove to the main corridor. He glanced behind him. There was no one nearby.

Dino was at the edge of panic. He pushed open the doors to the closest mall entrance to the bank, now only yards ahead. He had wanted to get to his target outside of the mall, preferably as he got out of his car, and grab his briefcase. A rap on the head would have slowed the guy enough to let Dino escape. Maybe he should have aborted the plan, but what would he have told Angelo? Things were getting out of control, but he *had* to stop the guy before he reached the main corridor or he'd lose the briefcase. He reached for his gun, a .32 caliber semi-automatic.

A quick move, the gun against the man's back, a single shot from the silenced pistol. The man started to fall; Dino grabbed him by the armpits before he totally collapsed.

"You alright, man?" He said it loud enough for anyone nearby to hear.

The man groaned and went limp.

Dino felt the man's weight sink into his arms. He managed to hold onto the gun while he struggled to keep the man from crumbling, talking to him as if he was a heart attack victim. He then pocketed the gun to keep it out of view from people walking nearby. He propped the limp man against the wall, grabbed the man's briefcase, and pulled out his cell phone. He feigned a 9-1-1 call as a passerby came close, who only shook his head and kept walking, not stopping to help. Dino cursed as he pushed at his loosened mustache. Heart pounding, he picked up the briefcase and stood up. Had anyone *really* seen what happened?

He gasped, "Oh shit." A woman stared at him from across the main corridor. Had she gotten a good look? How long had she been there? She kept looking at him with her mouth open. A chill went up his spine. *Does she know me? I can't let her get away, I just can't.* Terror gripped his heart at the possibility of being identified. *Who the hell is she?*

Fear crowded into his thoughts. *I had to kill the guy, didn't I? He was only seconds from the front of the bank. What else could I have done?*

It took Dino only a second to abandon leaving the mall by the side entrance, even though it was closest to his car. No, he *had* to get to the witness - just had to. With a tight grip on the briefcase, he started up the wide corridor toward the main entrance. He had to find her and stop her. Someone yelled something unintelligible behind him. Dino didn't look back. He cursed under his breath. He had been told only to retrieve whatever the man was carrying; it'd be most likely a briefcase or a leather satchel. He realized shooting the man had most certainly been a risky and foolish thing, but there had only been seconds to spare. He'd have to explain it, but would Angelo understand?

He moved quickly through the crowd. No one paid attention to him, no one but *her*. He saw that she was almost running, darting glances back toward him, and heading for the main entrance. *Where did I see that face? Gotta catch up to her. Maybe out in the parking lot... I can't leave a witness. Does she know me? That face...where?*

She was running now. Dino picked up his pace. "Get the hell outa my way." He shouldered through the crowd. He saw her dart to the entrance. He turned to cross the corridor to follow her, but a rush of noisy teenagers slowed him. Finally, he was at the door and pushed it open.

"*What the hell,*" he muttered. "*Who's he?*" Dino slowed as the woman approached a man and they walked toward the cars. "*A friend just happens to leave the mall same time she does?*" he mumbled. "*What're the fuckin' odds of that?*" He saw her get into a car, the man getting in the driver's seat.

Feeling helpless, his heart pounding, he turned and rushed along the sidewalk to the south end of the mall and then to the east side and on to his car. He started the engine and drove rapidly to where he had seen the woman and man get into a blue Chevy Malibu. *Would they still be parked there?* Driving up an adjacent aisle, he spotted them and pulled into an empty parking spot. *What should he do?*

He was certain she had recognized him. The shocked look on her face had said it all. Then a realization dawned on him. *That face. What the hell's her name? Christ, isn't she the niece of Roy Wilson? Sure. That's where I saw her.* He wiped the sweat from his brow. *I'll have to get rid of her. What else can I do? She saw me. This place will be crawling with cops any second. Better not stick around. Get her later.* He started the car. *Gotta find out where she lives.* He knew he didn't dare tell Angelo there had been a witness. No, that would be the end of him. He'd be a loose end they couldn't afford. He would have to take care of the problem himself and quickly, but not here.

—

The trip to the mall hadn't been a total waste of time, Tim thought. He'd been able to purchase a nice leather wallet. However, the tooled-leather briefcase he had ordered hadn't arrived as promised. The old and well-worn briefcase he had for years had become an embarrassment. He was on his own now, doing consulting work for large electronic companies in the Boston area. He recently splurged on new suits, new shoes and the custom tooled briefcase. The recent haircut, shorter now, more in style, augmented his clean-cut business look. Appearance counted for a lot in the face-to-face consulting business.

He glanced at his watch before turning to leave the mall and allowed he had time to grab a bite to eat. He stopped in at Rossetti's, where he purchased a slice of pepperoni pizza and a soda. The standup lunchtime crowd in the small and narrow shop was close and uncomfortable with hardly a spot to place his drink. Whiffs of perfume, aftershave, and body odor mixed with that of pizza overwhelmed his senses. Even though the sight of attractive eye-candy interested him, he ate quickly and departed.

Tim stepped through the west-entrance of the mall and into the sunshine, glad to be out of the crowded and noisy environment. He was pleased at the warm spring day after the cold snowy winter of 2009. The parking lot had filled and now only the distant rows were empty. He pulled the car keys from his pocket, stepped off the curb, and then clicked the button on the fob to sound the horn and flash the lights. He saw his car 150 feet away. He went to the crosswalk, waited for the cars to stop for him, and then started down the nearest isle.

"Pardon me, sir."

Startled, Tim turned to see an attractive woman hurrying toward him on his right. "Yes?"

"Would you please escort me to my car?"

He saw she was carrying only her purse. "Uh, sure. Where's your car?"

"Three rows over on the left, toward the back. Please, don't look back. Just hurry."

The fear in her voice was palpable. He stole a glance at her. Mid twenties, light brown hair, medium height and 120 pounds maybe. Another glance confirmed his initial observation: attractive, statuesque, and dressed in expensive threads.

"What's wrong?" Tim glanced behind him. "Someone stalking you?"

She wasn't able to walk fast in high heels and stumbled a few times. "Let's just hurry. Please." She sounded frantic.

"My car is just on the other isle, the blue Chevy Malibu. See it?" He pointed. "We can sit there. I don't think anyone would bother you in my car, and they wouldn't get your license number."

She stopped and looked boldly at him for a second. "Okay."

They walked to the next isle on their right and to the Malibu. He opened the passenger door and she sat down, pulling the door closed quickly. Tim hurried to the other side while looking around, but saw no one following. *What the hell is her problem?*

He sat down, closed the door, and pressed the door-lock button. "I didn't see anyone coming this way. You okay?"

She nodded.

He could see fear in her eyes as she turned around to look out the rear window.

"Nobody is going to bother you in here," said Tim, not at all sure he believed himself. He saw her lip quiver. "Can you tell me what's wrong?"

"I... I saw a murder," she said in a whisper. "He saw me."

"In the mall?" Tim couldn't stifle his shock. He stared at her wide-eyed.

She nodded. "Just a few minutes ago…and…he saw me."

"The killer saw you? He knows you?"

"He saw me."

At a loss, Tim held out his hand. "I'm Tim Beckman."

She hesitated, and then shook his hand. "Jennifer Wilson."

They saw flashing blue lights as several police cruisers sped into the west entrance of the parking lot. They stopped at the mall entrance and blocked the access road. Sirens were heard approaching.

—

Dino pulled in behind *Shorty's,* a dingy neighborhood bar he frequented, just inside Woburn. Shorty's pudgy wife, Ellen, spotted Dino coming through the doorway and reached for a bottle of cheap whiskey.

"Dino. You up early or is this a night cap?" She grinned. "Don't see you this time of day."

Dino scowled. "Yeah, had things to do."

"You look like shit. You sleep in those clothes?" She placed the shot glass on the bar.

Dino pulled a stool out from the bar and sat. "Got a beer to go with that?" He ignored her insults. He tossed the whisky down.

She filled a frosty mug and placed it in front of him. "Tryin' to get your motor started?"

"Yeah." He scowled and tipped the mug to his lips; then tried to stifle a belch. "Mind if I go out back, look at your phone books, and make a few calls?"

"Your cell phone dead?"

"Low battery. I need to look up a number. Not sure what the name is. It's a local call."

"Better be. Shorty don't like giving freebies. By the way, they stopped giving out phone books a while back. Where you been? Got the old books, though."

Dino slid off the barstool. "That might work. Be right back."

Ellen gave a halfhearted wave, her fleshy arm swaying.

—

"I guess the people now in the mall will have to answer some questions," remarked Tim. "Maybe you should tell the cops what you saw, huh?"

She looked at him wide-eyed. "No. No, I can't."

"Maybe you better tell *me,* then."

Jennifer looked at Tim for a few seconds in alarm, and then spoke. "He... he saw me. I recognized him. He knows I saw him."

"You can tell them who it is. The cops can protect you while they get him."

She shook her head. "No. He's connected. He'll get to me. I... I can't go to the cops."

Tim's uneasiness increased. He looked around at the other cars. "If he followed you, the shooter isn't in the mall any longer. Cops won't find him in there. He's out here somewhere or he's long gone."

Jennifer looked out the back window. Her lip trembled. "He's looking for me, isn't he?"

"He won't stick around with the cops here. He might have gotten my license number."

Jennifer looked at Tim with eyes wide. "He'll come after you?"

"He'll be looking for *you*. Maybe report back to his boss that you were in my car."

"More cop cars are coming in." Jennifer pointed to several police cruisers that were moving towards the southern entrance.

"Can't be sure, but I think the ambulance went around to the southeast doorway," said Tim.

"That's where the shooting was…at the bank entrance. That's where I saw him."

"Cops will be questioning everybody before they let them out," said Tim. "They'll be looking at the recordings from the cameras, also."

Jennifer's hand went to her mouth. "Oh, God. They'll see I was there."

"Yeah, me too," said Tim. "But there were a lot of people in the place."

"They'll see it was me…and you. Won't they?"

Tim nodded. "Eventually. Meanwhile, there'll be lots of people studying those videos."

Jennifer looked out the back window, a deep frown on her forehead.

"Why don't we go next door to the office park? It's all part of the mall parking lot. We can see what's going on at the entrance you mentioned."

She nodded. "Okay."

He stopped the car amongst the hundreds of vehicles in the office park, just east and part of the mall itself. From their new vantage point they could see some of the activity at the southeast mall doorway. Two ambulances and an EMT van were parked there.

"Maybe he'll give up looking for you," said Tim.

"Hope so. By the way, what do you do?"

"I'm an engineering consultant and an author."

A smile played at the corners of her mouth. "An author? Really?"

"Uh-huh. Mostly do consulting though. It's interesting and pays well."

"You've a family, girlfriend?"

"Parents live in Atlantic City," said Tim. "Never been married. Girlfriend hasn't answered my call in a week. Guess she isn't too thrilled with my spending so much time at the computer. But I have to make a living."

"What does she do?"

"She's in sales at DeGrasse Tools."

"What do *you* do?"

"I used to be an administrative assistant at a finance company in Woburn."

"You quit there?"

She nodded. "The guy I worked for was a real letch – hard to take. Didn't have much choice but to leave."

"Sorry."

Jennifer shrugged.

"You're not working right now?"

She shook her head. "You say you're self employed?"

"Uh-huh. I get a consulting job now and then working with larger electronic companies. I help them prepare proposals mostly. They pay well.

I stay busy. Otherwise, I write novels, and that hardly pays at all. You're married?" asked Tim.

She opened her left hand on her lap. "Not any longer." There were no rings on her fingers.

"If you want, I can follow you home. I mean, if you want me too." He glanced at her. "Check the place out. Make sure no one's there." It was a bold thing to say, but he didn't want her to just disappear from his life.

She looked at him for a few seconds before responding. "That'd be nice."

"We'll wait a while longer, until the cops go away from the entrances. Then, I'll drive you back to your car and follow you."

She nodded. "Okay."

It was forty minutes later when they went back to the west side of the mall. The police cruisers were gone and traffic seemed normal. They hadn't confided much in each other. Tim had tried to keep conversation going, but she kept herself well guarded with only occasional remarks. He turned the radio on to local news and they hid behind the monotonous drone of the broadcaster.

They parked for several minutes by her car while Tim looked for a possible ambush. No one seemed to be watching. He wanted to help her, but how?

"I don't see anyone suspicious," said Tim.

Jennifer turned to face him. "I really would feel a lot safer if you followed me."

Tim nodded, happy at her confidence in him. "Okay. I should look inside your place before you go in – make sure there's no one there."

"He... He knows where I live?" she asked.

"Maybe, by now."

Tim didn't think anyone had followed them. He parked behind her car at her Lowell apartment. She unlocked the door and let him enter. Tim did a quick check of each room and returned to the doorway.

"Doesn't look like anyone's been here. You'll be okay."

"Thanks." Jennifer stepped inside, held the door open and looked at him. "I'm afraid to stay here."

"You have a friend you can stay with for a couple days, let this blow over?"

She shook her head. "He saw me. By now he remembers me and knows who I am."

"He *knows* you?"

"I saw him once. It was at a party at my uncle's place. He probably remembers me."

"Oh shit." He saw her lip tremble. "You want to call the police?"

She shook her head. "He won't want to have a witness able to identify him. He'll be coming after me right away. It's how they work."

Tim's eyes widened. "*They?*"

She looked at him and nodded. "My uncle has some connected friends."

"And there's no one that'll put you up until maybe the cops get this guy?"

She shook her head slowly. "I couldn't put my friends in danger. Cops aren't likely to catch this guy."

"Staying here doesn't sound like a good idea."

"I've been house sitting for my parents. Their condo is in a gated community in Chelmsford. I could go there."

"It'd be better than here, but still..."

She blinked back tears. "He would find me...wouldn't he?"

Tim nodded slowly.

A tear broke loose and wet her cheek. "Would you drive me there? And... and stay with me...until morning?"

His heart went out to her. She was distractingly beautiful and vulnerable. He wondered what he was getting himself into. *They are connected,* echoed in his ear.

"Okay. Let's not hang here."

Jennifer hurried down the hall as Tim stood by the door and looked around the living room. A framed picture of an older couple, likely her parents, he thought, sat on top of a bookcase. A stack of magazines was on the bottom shelf. The place was picked up and neat.

A few minutes later, Jennifer appeared with a carry-on type bag. "This'll hold me for a few days."

"Okay. We'll go." Tim opened the door and looked across the parking lot. "No one out here." He stepped out and she followed, closing and locking the door.

CHAPTER 2

Dino flipped through the pages of the well-worn area phone book. *Damn, must be a million Wilson's here. What the hell's her name?* His finger went down the page as he glanced at every name listed. When he got to the end, he cursed. *Goddamned Roy Wilson is here, but what the hell is her name?*

He pulled another beat up phone book from the stack. It had the Chelmsford listings. He found the section for Wilson and started down the list. His finger stopped at Wilson, Jennifer. *Yeah. That's got to be her. Jennifer. Yeah, that was her name.*

He scribbled down her name, address and phone number. He pulled out his phone from his jacket pocket, saw he still had a small charge in the battery, and dialed the number. He let it ring six times and hung up. *I'm gonna pay you a visit.* He stuffed the note in his shirt pocket and went back out to the bar.

Ellen grinned. "What's the matter, she stood you up?"

"You're really funny," Dino scowled. "Pour me another shot, gotta chase this beer down."

Ellen reached for the bottle of cheap stuff and poured a shot glass. "So, what have you been up to? Staying outa jail?"

"Keeping busy. Little jobs to pay the rent." Dino tossed the whiskey down in one gulp.

"Bob was in here a couple days ago. Hadn't seen him in a while."

"Downy? What the hell he want?"

Ellen shrugged. "He didn't say. I didn't ask."

—

"Could we stop and get a bite to eat?" said Jennifer. "There isn't much at my parent's place."

"Sure. Want to stop at *Marty's*? It's just before we get to Chelmsford," replied Tim, happy to spend more time with her.

"Okay. I've never been there." She turned toward Tim. "You think we'll be safe?"

Tim shrugged. "I don't know where the shooter is. All I know is that you were a witness. We'll have to be on our toes." He tried not to show the nervousness he felt. He wasn't at all sure he wasn't getting into a difficult situation. *Certainly different than my usual existence.* Her arousing good looks had won him over.

Jennifer stayed silent until they arrived at the restaurant, and he left her to her own thoughts. The restaurant was set back in a large parking lot. Tim looked at the cars but didn't see anyone suspicious.

"I've been here a few times," said Tim. "Food is good. Kinda wild on Friday and Saturday nights."

"I've had enough *wild* for a while."

Tim pulled open the door and they went in. They were shown to a seat near the entrance. Jennifer ordered a salad and Tim a cheeseburger. Nervous small talk occupied the time until their food arrived. He caught her staring at him, her gray-green eyes searching his face.

Tim reached for the ketchup bottle. "You recognized this guy from a party at your uncle's?"

"Roy invited nearly everyone he knew for this big bash of a lawn party," said Jennifer. "This guy, I didn't get his name, kept staring at me and made me uncomfortable. I thought at the time, he was just some gopher my uncle used for errands. I should have known better, as my ex-husband was there also."

"I thought you said they didn't get along – your ex and your uncle."

"They tolerated each other, but the past year they really split apart." She frowned and looked away. "I shouldn't be talking out of school. I barely know you."

"We can talk about something else." He felt the tingle of excitement when he looked at her and heard her voice. He wanted to know her, whatever the risk.

Jennifer smiled. "Oh, hell, I have to talk to somebody. Uncle Roy has a real problem with the business Bob, my ex, is in. My uncle isn't above grabbing something that's not his, if the occasion presents itself. But I've never heard of him condoning murder and blackmail, which is what I've come to believe is my ex's expertise."

"They both work in the Cipriano outfit?" asked Tim.

Jennifer didn't reply right away. "Roy's a real estate developer mainly in Florida and Las Vegas. I don't know what he does for the mob. He's not a made guy. Probably handles some of their property investments."

"Cipriano?"

"I've never seen them together..."

"And your ex?"

Jennifer scowled. "He runs an investment business, mainly. But he is also involved in real estate deals. I think it's all part of a moneymaking scheme for the Cipriano outfit. He's no made-guy either. But, he'll do anything they ask of him, hoping to get in better. But they probably don't trust him. I surely wouldn't."

"Sounds like he's a real piece-of-work."

"He is that."

———

Dino dialed the number from his car as he watched the apartment. There was a car parked in the assigned slot, but he hadn't seen any movement at the windows. It was getting to be early evening, but there weren't any lights on. The telephone rang, but nobody answered. He hung up after six rings.

"Is she in there or did she leave with that guy in the Malibu?" he asked himself as he pondered the risk of breaking into the apartment. He knew if she was there and just not answering the phone, she'd be able to get off a 9-1-1 call before he even had her door open. Just then his phone buzzed.

"Yeah?"

"This is Burt."

"Yeah, man. Got something?" said Dino.

"You wanted details on the tag, right?"

"Yeah. What'd you get?"

"Guys name is Tim Beckman. He's got a place in Lowell."

Dino pulled out a pen and the now crumpled paper with Jennifer's address. "Okay, give it to me."

Burt read off Tim's address and phone number. "Are we good?"

"Yeah, thanks. I'll make it up to you." Dino closed the phone and started the car.

—

It was dusk when Tim and Jennifer left Marty's. She gave him directions to her parent's condo located in a gated residential area in Chelmsford.

"Your parents are where? Europe?" asked Tim.

"Uh-huh. Visiting friends in Italy," replied Jennifer.

"How long will they be gone?"

"They've been gone two weeks. Six more to go."

"And you're house sitting?"

"I've been stopping in here every few days," said Jennifer. "They like me to air the place out and water the plants." She handed Tim the remote key card. "Just hold it up to the windshield."

When he did, the large black steel gate swung open, then closed when he was just past it. "It won't keep out a sophisticated burglar or badass, but it'll slow them down," said Tim.

"How long...?"

Tim shrugged. "Maybe a day or two, if he wants to play it safe and replicate the gate card. For a real badass, he'll climb over the fence. I don't know what we're dealing with here."

"If it's the guy I think it is, he's not all that bright."

"We'll stay alert," said Tim.

———

Dino drank the last of the coffee, tossed the cup onto the junk littering the back seat, and then looked at his watch. "Two goddamn hours. Where the hell are they?"

From where he parked, he had a good view of the apartment and parking area, dark except for the sodium vapor lamps casting a sickly orange pall over the parked cars. Dino's mood had gotten fouler by the hour since the event at the mall. He worried about reporting to Angelo, as he knew he'd have to admit there was a witness. He wanted to eliminate this threat before having to report, but was overdue. He'd have to call soon.

He called Beckman's phone. It rang three times.

"Hello."

"Yeah, looking for Steve." There was no light on in the apartment. *Maybe the guy has a cell phone, but where is he?*

"There's no Steve here. You have the wrong number."

"Sorry." Dino closed the phone.

Shit. Where the hell is he? Back at her place?

He looked at the scrap of paper, then dialed Jennifer's apartment. The phone rang ten times before he hung up.

Fear crept into his thoughts. *He had to find her; couldn't tell Angelo he left a witness. Where were they?* He opened the cell phone. He didn't dare wait any longer to make his report. He dialed the number Angelo had given him.

"Yeah?"

"It's me. Checking in from my, ah, errand."

"You just callin' *now*? What the hell you been doin'?" said Angelo. "Already got the news from the TV. What'd you do, off the guy?"

"I...it didn't go as I planned."

"You freakin' killed the guy?"

"I got into a kind of problem," said Dino. "Been trying to fix it."

Angelo spoke slow and forceful. "You bringin' me a problem? I send you out to grab a satchel and you're bringing me a problem? Is that what I'm hearin'?"

"It wasn't a clean deal."

"What? You got made?"

"Yeah. Been trying to fix it."

"Fix it? What fix it?" Angelo's voice rose in pitch and volume. "Why'd you pop the guy? And now you also have a witness?"

"I... I can fix this problem."

"Is that what you're doin' now?"

"Yeah. Waiting at one of the sites."

"You dumb shit. Get away from there. Get your ass back here. You got the package?"

"Yeah."

"I gotta call the boss. He ain't gonna like this."

"I... I can fix this," stuttered Dino.

"Get your ass back here!"

———

Jennifer frowned. "Who was that on your phone?"

Tim shook his head and looked at the cell phone screen. "It's a blocked number."

"Was it him?"

"Guy looking for a Steve. Could of been him, I guess. Maybe he thought he was calling my apartment phone."

"I'm scared. He probably already checked my apartment and yours," said Jennifer.

"I hope he doesn't make a connection to this place anytime soon."

"Let's turn the TV on, see if there is anymore news about it," suggested Jennifer.

When the 11 o'clock news came on they stayed on a local news channel. Barely a minute was devoted to the incident at the Tri-City Mall with only a few photos of the mall area.

"The cops are keeping it quiet for now," said Tim. "They did say the dead guy is an accountant employed by Century Design, an investment firm."

Jennifer brought her hand to her mouth. "That...that's my ex's company."

"You didn't recognize the man that got shot?"

She shook her head. "I... I was looking at the shooter."

"Why would they kill an accountant...and who?"

"There were several working there for a head accountant, but I don't remember his name." Jennifer clicked off the TV and looked at Tim. "I'm really tired. I have to get some sleep."

"Did you want me to stay? I can crash on this couch." *What am I doing? God, she's gorgeous.*

"Would you mind? I'd feel a lot safer."

Tim patted the cushion. "This'll be just fine."

Jennifer stood up. "There's a bathroom in the hallway, just to your right. I'm going to use the one in the master bedroom. You're going to be okay out here?"

"Sure. This throw blanket is all I need. I'll be fine," said Tim. *Should I stay awake?*

"I'd stay up...watch TV with you, but I'm wrung out."

"Get some sleep."

She nodded and smiled, then disappeared down the hallway.

Tim woke up with a start. The phone was ringing in the kitchen. After four rings it went to the answering machine, but nobody left a message. He looked at his watch: 12:08 and fell asleep. At 12:45 the phone rang, but again there was no message. Tim swore and went back to sleep. At 3am the phone rang again. Determined to find out who was calling, he sprung from under the blanket, left the couch, and darted to the kitchen. The caller had hung up.

When Tim started back toward the couch, he saw Jennifer standing at the end of the hall clasping a robe at her throat. "That's scaring me," she said softly. "Who...who is it?"

Tim shook his head. "Dunno. Keeps hanging up."

She stood there in her clinging robe, looking at him. He was suddenly aware of her beauty and vulnerability. His face felt hot. She took a few steps toward him and stopped. He went to her and pulled her gently against him. She leaned into him, burying her face against his shoulder, her arms around him while pressing her abdomen against his arousal. She backed slowly down the hall, tugging on his shirt.

CHAPTER 3

Dino pulled into the parking lot of Mario's Pizza. He was fearful. The job hadn't gone well – *that damn witness*. Meeting with Angelo Costello was going to be painful. He wouldn't be tolerant of the screw-up.

He picked up the briefcase and got out of his car. He took a deep breath and exhaled, then walked to the back door of Mario's. He knocked several times. When it opened, he went into the back room located opposite the walk-in freezer. Dino was surprised and a chill went up his back to see Angelo seated with Robert Downy. Neither man was smiling. They both nodded in greeting. Angelo pointed to a chair.

Dino put the briefcase on the table and pushed it toward Angelo. "I... I can fix this. I can clean it up."

"Shut up!" said Angelo.

Dino sat back as if slapped.

Downy glared silently.

Angelo reached for the briefcase, opened it, and turned it upside down. The contents spilled onto the table. He picked up the cell phone, opened it, and looked at the screen as he pushed some of the buttons. Then he handed it to Downy who repeated the procedure, and then closed it and placed it on the table.

Downy scowled, looked at Angelo. "Nothing."

Angelo picked up the passport, thumbed through it, and passed it to Downy. Then he picked up an envelope, opened it, and withdrew a single airline ticket. He stared at it. "Son of a bitch," he growled and then handed it to Downy.

"Miami? What the hell?"

Angelo grinned. "You sending him on vacation?"

Downy didn't smile. "It's a one-way. No connecting flight. What was he up to?"

"He coulda got a connection down there to anywhere: Aruba, Grenada, Panama, anywhere."

"What else you got?" growled Downy.

Angelo pushed aside a calculator, and then picked up two CDs in plastic cases. He stared at them for a few seconds, and then handed them to Downy. "Marked 3 and 4. Whatever that means."

Downy looked at them and turned to Angelo. "Where's number 1 and 2?"

Angelo searched through the pockets of the briefcase and shrugged. "Empty."

Downy reached down alongside his chair and pulled up a computer bag. He slid a laptop onto the table and flipped open the display. "We'll take a look."

The computer booted and was ready to use in a minute. Dino glanced from Angelo to Downy, nervously biting his lip. Downy selected the CD marked number 3 and inserted it into the drive-slot. Angelo leaned toward him and looked at the screen.

"A spreadsheet," observed Angelo.

Downy scanned down the sheet. "Shit! These are all my accounts."

Angelo stared at the screen. "What accounts? Whose?"

"Oh, Christ. It looks like...it is...the Vegas accounts."

"Names?"

"Yeah, names, money, everything," exclaimed Downy. He ejected the CD and inserted the one-marked 4.

"Another spreadsheet," declared Angelo.

"Freakin' hell. This one has all the public investment accounts. Son of a bitch!" Downy glared at Angelo. "Where was Owens going with this? Where's number 1 and 2? What the hell is going on here?"

Angelo shifted his stare to Dino. "You bring everything? Take anything outa the briefcase?"

"You got everything, Ang. I never even opened the thing."

Angelo glared. "Owens was headed toward the bank, right?"

Dino nodded. "Yeah. Walking right towards it when I stopped him."

Downy looked at Angelo. "He could have been taking these CDs to his safe deposit box. Maybe number 1 and 2 are in there. God knows what's on them."

"Yeah," said Angelo. "Coulda been going to the bank to leave these two CDs and get some traveling money from his safe deposit box." Angelo glared at Dino. "We sure as hell can't ask him now can we, since you fuckin' killed him?"

"God damn it," exclaimed Downy. "Owens left early. I was walking by his desk and the phone was ringing. I picked it up, figured on taking a message. But son-of-a-bitch, if it wasn't a call from a travel agent. Just pure luck, or I'd a never known about this. I looked on his computer and saw where he had copied shit to CDs. I knew I had to stop him. I saw him walk out with that briefcase of his." He looked at Angelo. "I had to call you, to stop him somehow and get that damn briefcase. Christ, this could bring it all down on our heads."

"Well, that ain't gonna happen." Angelo glanced at Dino. "Except now we got ole Dino here screwing up big-time. What the hell happened?"

Dino gulped. A bead of sweat was already on his brow. His shirt clung to his body.

Angelo's fist came down on the table and Dino jumped. "Talk, damn you! What the hell happened? It was a simple assignment. Grab the fuckin' briefcase. That was the assignment. Just grab the goddamn thing!"

"He... He got ahead of me in traffic. I had to hurry, but I didn't catch up to him until I entered the mall. I got to him just inside. He was almost to the bank...had to stop him. I shot him in the back. There was no visible blood; his jacket covered everything. I pretended he was drunk when a guy came by, and I propped him against the wall. I didn't think anyone really saw what happened. I took the briefcase and was going to leave the way I came in. That's when I saw her."

"And the broad saw you, that it?" demanded Angelo.

Dino nodded. "She acted scared. Stared, like she recognized me. When she started to run toward the west exit, I followed her trying to catch up. I wanted to take care of her outside before she got in her car. But then some dude joined her and they went to *his* car. I couldn't get to them safely, and I wanted to leave before the cops shut everything down. I was gonna look her up later...and take her out then."

"You were, were you?" yelled Angelo "Who the hell said for you to do that?"

"I just figured..."

"No one authorized a hit on *anyone*, you dumb shit! The plan was to grab the damn briefcase. That was the plan. Not start World War-3." Angelo, his face red, shook his head. "I can't freakin' believe this." He glared at Dino. "And then what happened?"

Dino took a deep breath. "I kept trying to find them. She was with this guy. Then you called me back here."

"You screwed up. You didn't do as we planned. You fuckin' killed a guy. This is on you."

Dino nodded. He realized Angelo was a made man in the Cipriano family, and not one to forgive such amateurish performance.

Downy looked at Dino and asked calmly, "You think you know the woman?"

"I'm pretty sure I saw her at some lawn party at Roy Wilson's place a year ago."

Downy looked at Angelo. "Jennifer Wilson is his niece. Coulda been her."

Angelo shook his head, glared at Dino, and raised his voice. "Get the hell outa here, you goddamn moron. This is on you. Stay in town. This ain't over yet."

Dino backed up in his chair, nearly tipping it over. He beat a hasty retreat, surprised to be alive.

CHAPTER

4

The wall-phone rang while they ate breakfast. Jennifer looked at Tim. "I have to answer it, might be my parents." She lifted the handset and stretched the cord to reach her seat at the table. "Hello."

Tim watched her as she listened. *God, last night was so marvelous.*

"Uncle Roy, I don't know what you're talking about." She listened again. "Yes, I *was* at that mall yesterday, but I have no idea what you're getting at. I didn't see anything out of the ordinary." Again, she listened. "What was it I was supposed to see?" She clamped her lips together as the other party spoke. "Uncle Roy, I don't know anything. I didn't see anything. You don't believe me?" She shook her head and glanced at Tim. "Why would anyone come after me? It's got to be mistaken identity." Again, she clamped her lips together. "I've been here. You know, I promised to keep an eye on the place. I'll be leaving in a while and go home." She nodded. "Okay. Anything happens, I'll call you." She stood up and hung up the phone. When she turned back to the table, her eyes were tearing up. She sat down, took a sip of coffee, and wiped her eyes with the back of her hands. "I hate lying to him."

"Want to tell me about it?" he asked.

She hesitated, but in a few seconds, started. "My uncle, Roy Wilson, is a real estate developer in Florida and Las Vegas. He's connected with all kinds of strange characters." She paused, and then looked at Tim. "The shooter I saw in the mall was someone I've seen at my uncle's place, a lawn party last year."

"You didn't sound happy to be talking with him."

"

She shook her head. "This guy, the shooter, probably recognized me. Somehow my uncle heard about it. He's angry that I won't tell him. Maybe, I should've."

"You're his niece. Would he let anyone hurt you? Would *he* hurt you?"

She looked down at her plate, toying with her food. When she looked up, her eyes glistened. Her lip trembled. "I don't know. It may be out of his hands."

"What did he say to you?" asked Tim.

"He said he got a call last night about an incident at Tri-City Mall. He wanted to know what I had seen there. He said some one saw me there, and that I witnessed an incident. He insisted I tell him what I saw."

"You didn't tell him..."

She shook her head. "No. I couldn't. I'm afraid of what might happen to me. He...he seems like a nice man, but long ago I concluded that he was into the mob up to his eyeballs and has been involved in illegal stuff. FBI came here one day and talked to my parents about him, some investigation."

"Your dad...is he...?" he started, looking for the right words not to offend.

She shook her head. "No. He's a straight arrow. He made his fortune legitimately in commercial construction, both here and overseas. His brother, of course, Uncle Roy, he tried to influence my dad to do things for him, but my dad wouldn't hear of it. They don't talk much anymore. See each other on a holiday, sometimes."

"Do you want to talk to your father about this...what you saw, your uncle?" asked Tim.

She pursed her lips. "Don't want to. They deserve their peace. But I might have to."

"What do you want to do? Talk to the police? FBI?"

She shook her head. "I don't know." She stared at her food, and then looked up at him.

He saw the tears well up again. He got up and went to her, tugged her out of her chair, and embraced her. She cried softly. He caressed her silky hair. Her arms tightened around him. In a few minutes she quieted. He guided her to the couch in the living room and they sat together, his arm around her shoulders.

"My uncle can't protect me; he owes his soul to those gangsters. I'm afraid to tell my father, don't want him dragged into it. And besides, what could he do?"

"And the law?" he asked.

Her eyes widened. "If I say anything, they'll want me to testify, to be a witness." She shook her head vigorously. "I'd be dead." She looked at him, grimacing. "*They* know I saw him. *They* know who I am. They're going to kill me." Her lip trembled.

He pulled her against him. "We can't let that happen." He grinned. "I'm getting to like you." He knew then that he meant it despite the nervousness he felt about the situation he was getting into. Was he being reckless, he wondered? His last girlfriend no longer returned his calls; maybe it was a blessing.

She touched his face, looked into his eyes. "I can't believe I met someone like you."

He held her silently for a minute and then asked, "You have to be at work? Someone will miss you?"

She shook her head. "No. I haven't worked after my divorce. I have some money squirreled away and my parents help me when I need it."

"Will someone come looking for you?" he asked.

"I have a few girl friends that'll call for lunch or drinks. There's a couple guys call every other week looking for a date." She wrinkled her nose. "There's only you – right now."

Tim smiled, "I kinda like that."

She leaned into him. "Me, too."

Jennifer turned on the TV. "Maybe they'll have something about...about what happened."

"It should at least bring some mention, I would think," said Tim.

Ten minutes passed and then brief comments about the killing at Tri-City Mall were presented. The deceased was reported to be Edward Owens, late fifties, employed at Century Design, an investment company. The assailant had not been identified, but the Burlington police were going through the video footage from mall cameras and requested any witness to the event to call them; promising their anonymity would be preserved.

Jennifer looked at Tim and shook her head. "If it goes to trial, they'd subpoena me as a witness. There's no anonymity. Also, any leak at the police or DA could allow me to be identified and I'd be dead – never make it to trial."

"Maybe you should stay here at your parent's place for the time being," suggested Tim.

"Safer than my apartment?"

"Not by much, but it *is* gated," said Tim. "Be careful who you open the door to."

Jennifer handed her cell phone to him. "Please put your cell number in my contact list...just in case."

"Okay. But don't open the door to anyone you don't know."

She wrapped her arms around him and kissed him. "I kinda like you."

"Like you too."

CHAPTER 5

Tim left Jennifer at her parent's condo and drove to his apartment in Lowell. He had to admit the night before with Jennifer had been wonderful. He wanted to see a lot more of her. His current squeeze hadn't called back; maybe that was fortunate. He showered and changed clothes; pressed khaki pants and a button down blue shirt. While the coffee maker did its thing, he decided to call his friend Bruce Engelman, a freelance crime reporter who sold most of his work to the **Boston Eagle**. Tim had met Bruce while both attended University of Massachusetts Lowell years ago. Bruce could likely shed light on the mall incident and was as trustworthy as they came. Although Bruce didn't talk much about the work he did, Tim was certain he knew his way around the dark corridors and corners of organized crime in the northern suburbs of Boston. He called Bruce and they agreed to have lunch at Roscoe's in Burlington.

They met in the foyer, then went in and asked for a booth. Even though it was the lunch hour, they were able to get a booth in a few minutes.

"So, Tim, what's with all the mystery?" Bruce grinned from ear to ear. "You don't buy lunch, especially here, if something isn't on your mind. So, what gives?"

Tim let out his breath slowly. "What do you know about the incident at the Tri-City Mall the other day?"

Bruce shrugged. "What I read in the paper. Why?"

They paused as the waiter took their order. Both requested a burger and fries and a beer. When the waiter walked away, Tim looked at Bruce. "You don't know the people involved?"

Bruce nodded. "Sure. Dead guy's Edward Owens. He was working at Century Design, an investment company. He's an accountant."

"What do you think got him killed?" asked Tim.

"Who knows? Haven't heard." Bruce grinned. "So, what's with the questions? Come on, what are you into? This ain't your line of work."

Tim sighed. "This is all confidential, right?"

Bruce frowned. "You gotta ask?"

"Just say it. I want to hear it."

Bruce shook his head. "Yeah, it's all confidential...for now."

"There was a witness to the shooting."

Bruce's eyes widened, his voice dropped. "You...you saw it?" He leaned closer.

Tim shook his head. "No, not me. Friend of mine."

"Went to the cops, yet?"

"No. This person is scared to be exposed."

Bruce nodded, but waited until the server placed the beer mugs in front of them. "Yeah, I understand that, but they're bound to find out about it eventually. Bad situation." Bruce met Tim's gaze. "Can't your friend just forget about it?"

Tim shook his head. "She was spotted by the shooter."

"She?" Bruce raised an eyebrow, a grin started at the corner of his mouth.

"Never mind," Tim scowled. "She's scared shitless."

Bruce frowned. "What aren't you telling me? She can just ignore it, can't she?"

Conversation ceased while the waiter placed their food on the table. Tim and Bruce passed the salt and pepper shakers and squirted ketchup on the fries. Then Tim looked up at Bruce.

"Shooter can identify her and she's seen him before."

"Shit," Bruce grimaced. "How? Her husband? What?"

"I think the shooter works for her ex-husband in some way. The ex and her uncle are connected."

"Come on. Gimme his name."

"Uncle is Roy Wilson, some kind of real estate tycoon," said Tim.

"Heard of him. Sleazy guy with Vegas connections."

"Yeah, well, someone might be leaning on him to give up his niece. Niece is denying she saw anything. However, the shooter knows she did."

Bruce shook his head. "So, who's the shooter?"

"She's seen him at her uncle's place, but doesn't know his name," said Tim.

Bruce took a bite out of his hamburger and chewed. "So, what do you want from me?" he finally asked.

"She opens her mouth, she's dead."

"Yeah, I'd say so," replied Bruce.

"She's afraid they'll come after her, that she poses too much of a threat to this guy, the shooter."

"She's probably right." Bruce took a long pull from his beer.

They looked at each other without speaking for a minute, and then Tim cleared his throat.

"Can you find out who is leaning on the uncle?"

Bruce scowled. "Sure, but then what? What kinda jam you gonna get your ass into?"

"Dunno. Just want to find out who the players are," said Tim halfheartedly. "I want to help her."

Bruce let out a long breath and sat back in his seat. "Look, I know these guys. Been sniffing their cologne for quite a while." He raised his eyebrows. "I do crime reporting, remember?"

Tim nodded. "Yeah. Figured you knew these guys."

"What I'm sayin' is that I can find out names, no problem. But what are you going to do with the information?" He shook his head. "You nose around on your own, you'll end up dead. They'll find the woman and that'll be the end of her, too."

Tim looked downhearted. "So, what you're saying is that you won't help me?"

Bruce leaned on the table and looked directly at Tim. "I'm not going to help you get yourself killed. You want to work *with* me; maybe we can figure something out."

Tim's eyes widened. "Yeah? What can we do? I *gotta* help her."

"First of all, who is *her*?"

"Jennifer Wilson, niece of Roy Wilson," said Tim.

"And where's she staying at the moment?"

"Her parents' condo in Chelmsford."

"Married? What?" asked Bruce.

"Recently divorced from a Robert Downy. She recognized the shooter as an acquaintance of her ex-husband. Saw them together at the uncle's place some time back."

Bruce shook his head. "Marvelous. This Downy guy is anything but good news. She may have more to fear from him than her uncle. He into high finance, right?"

Tim nodded. "Yeah, owns an investment firm...actually, it's Century Design."

Bruce rolled his eyes. "Ex-husband, uncle, shooters, they're all in the Cipriano organization."

"Shit…"

"Yep."

"What should I do?" asked Tim. "Gotta do *something*."

"I need a day to ask questions and sniff around," said Bruce. "Meantime, you keep her out of sight. Keep her calmed down."

"You gonna call me?"

"You'll hear from me."

CHAPTER 6

Tim used Jennifer's key card to access the gated lot where she was staying. At her door, he knocked lightly. He wanted her to see him at the peephole.

The door opened an inch and a teary eye looked out at him.

"I'm alone. Will you let me in?"

The door opened wider and Tim stepped inside pushing the door closed behind him. He saw her lip trembling, face still wet from crying. He reached out and put a hand on her arm, gently pulling her toward him.

"Something happen?"

"The phone keeps ringing." She sniffled. "Every 15-20 minutes. I'm afraid to answer it."

He held her against him.

"I'm glad you're back," she mumbled.

"Okay if I answer it next time?"

She looked at him, hesitated, and then nodded. "Yes."

When the phone rang, Tim picked it up. "Hello."

A no-nonsense voice replied. "I'd like to speak with Jennifer."

"She can't come to the phone right now."

"I want to speak with Jennifer. Put her on." The voice was insistent.

"She's indisposed," said Tim. "May I leave a message?"

"Alright, damn it. This is her uncle. I suggest she meet me at Sandy's restaurant at 4pm. Think she can handle that?"

"I will give her the message."

"Yeah, do that."

Tim checked his voice and e-mail while Jennifer showered and dressed. On the way to Sandy's they stopped at his apartment where he put on a blue blazer. He checked his USPS mail for bills that were soon due. She told Tim a little more of herself as they drove. She had gone to public school in Chelmsford, then to UML for a degree in Business Administration. At a dinner party shortly after graduation, she met Bob Downy and they were married a year later.

"What drew you to him?"

"He was a charmer and showered me with gifts. I guess I didn't see beyond that."

"What changed?"

"I became frightened of Bob with his extended absences, his shady friends, and his increasingly violent temper."

"Did he hurt you?"

"He would hit me in nearly every argument. I divorced him two years after I married him. I took my parent's name again, and lived there while getting my masters degree."

"I think you did a smart thing."

"I moved into my apartment six months ago when I got a position as an administrative assistant in a medical insurance company."

"Sounds like a good move."

"Not so much, unfortunately. The company went into downsize shortly thereafter."

"Sorry. I grew up in Lowell and went to UML where I met my friend Bruce. He was a journalism student."

"What is he doing now?"

"Bruce worked for the Eagle for several years and then went on his own as a free-lance investigative reporter specializing in crime, particularly that which occurred north of Boston."

"Sounds like an interesting guy."

"You'll like him."

"And what did you do in school?"

"I graduated with a degree in electronic engineering and found employment at Raytheon. After a few years, I focused on technical writing and proposal preparation. During that time, I had taken courses in communications, finance and management."

"So, where are you working now?"

"I just finished a large proposal job at Raytheon. I'm self-employed, do consulting at various electronic companies."

They parked near the front of Sandy's restaurant and went inside. Before the hostess asked to seat them, Jennifer spotted her uncle waving from a booth near the far end. "That's Roy Wilson, my uncle."

Tim saw a dapper well-dressed man of middle age with salt-pepper hair. He stood up as they approached.

Jennifer introduced Tim to her uncle and sat next to Tim in the booth.

Roy stared at Tim. "You're the young man on the phone?"

Tim nodded. "Yes."

He turned his attention to Jennifer. "You want him in on this conversation?"

"Yes. Tim's my friend."

Roy had a glass of wine in front of him. "I guess the least I can do is buy you guys supper," he said with a slight grin.

Jennifer shrugged. "Maybe a bite."

"Thanks," said Tim.

Jennifer asked for a small salad while Tim ordered a chiliburger. Both asked for a diet soda. Roy ordered a shrimp cocktail.

When Roy inquired about Jennifer's parents, she told him they would be in Europe for at least another month. Tim was becoming increasingly uncomfortable with Roy's frequent glances.

After the food arrived, Roy Wilson asked a few questions of Tim to which he gave brief responses. Roy went on to say, mostly to Tim, that he was fond of his niece and would never mean harm to her. He had heard through contacts that a shooting had occurred at the mall and that Jennifer had witnessed it. But what was worse, the shooter had recognized her. Roy said he had called her only to get her side of the story so he could corroborate what he had been told. He insisted that if he knew the whole story he could do something to make sure that Jennifer was not threatened or intimidated.

"How about *killed?*" she retorted.

Roy shook his head. "That's not going to happen."

Then she told him what she had seen and how Tim had helped her. She mentioned the shooter was a man that had been at her uncle's party a year earlier.

Roy nodded, then sat back and sipped his wine in apparent thought.

Jennifer toyed with her salad. Tim finished his food. The waitress brought the check and asked if there would be anything else. Roy smiled at her and said they were finished.

No one spoke for almost a minute, as Roy seemed to be distracted in thought. After their meals, Roy Wilson picked up the check and before sliding out of the booth, looked at Jennifer. "Can you stay out of sight for a couple days?"

Jennifer glanced at Tim. He nodded. "Yes," she replied.

"Good." He glanced at Tim then back to Jennifer. "Give me a couple days to take care of this problem. Nothing's going to happen to you."

Jennifer nodded, putting her arm through Tim's. Roy slid out of the booth and check in hand went toward the cashier and the exit.

"Dare I believe him?" asked Jennifer.

Tim raised his eyebrows. "I don't know what to expect. I guess we give him a couple days, see what happens." He started to get out of the booth and Jennifer followed.

CHAPTER 7

Angelo had called Dino and told him to meet at Mario's Pizza. Dino pulled into the parking lot and stopped close to the building. He saw three other cars in the lot, but none were Angelo's. He was afraid of another dressing down by Angelo Costello. It hadn't gone well the other night. What were they going to have him do?

Dino knew he had screwed up. He had started following the mark as soon as the man left Century Design. He'd been told to follow him and grab the briefcase or whatever he was carrying. Also, he wasn't to fail.

He didn't see Angelo's car, so he leaned back and lit a cigarette. *What the hell can I tell him? I screwed up, too much of a hurry.* His hand trembled. He wondered if they were going to hang him out to dry and have someone else take care of the witness. He lowered the window and blew the cigarette smoke into the night breeze.

Dino never heard the pop. The bullet entered just in front of his ear and a spray of blood and brain exploded from the other side of his head.

Angelo stepped back into the shadows of the building and overhanging trees and unscrewed the silencer. He walked the fifty feet to a maroon Chrysler 300, opened the trunk, and placed the silencer and pistol in a briefcase. He removed the leather gloves and tossed them in as well. He then pushed the trunk lid down to latch it.

In the car he took a moment to admire the plush interior. The vibrating phone in his shirt pocket startled him.

"Yeah?"

"The car okay?"

"Yeah," said Angelo, "Real nice car. Everything's fine. No problem."

"Okay. You know where I'll be."

"See you." Angelo closed the phone and pulled off the nylon mask, and stuffed it in his pocket.

He left the parking lot and turned toward the town of Woburn and Shorty's Lounge. He would change the plates back when he got there and return the car to the Chrysler dealer in the morning after he thoroughly wiped it down.

The next morning Tim and Jennifer watched local TV news as an announcement was made of the assassination of Dino Ferrero, a known low-level mob figure. Jennifer, excited, turned to Tim. "That's the guy I saw – the shooter."

"You're sure?"

"Yes. I won't forget that face. He had a phony mustache the other day, wasn't even on straight."

Tim's cell phone buzzed. He saw that it was Bruce calling. "Hello."

"I guess you saw it on the TV?"

"We're watching it right now. Better we don't talk about it on the phone."

"Could you both meet me for lunch at 11:30 at Leon's Diner in North Chelmsford?" asked Bruce.

"Sure. Something comes up, I'll call you."

Tim helped Jennifer out of the car and spotted Bruce walking toward them across the parking lot. Bruce was dressed in his signature jeans and sweatshirt.

"Jennifer, this is Bruce, friend I was telling you about."

She gave him a smile. "Nice to meet you."

Jennifer had her arm through Tim's and looked about uneasily.

"How come you picked this place," asked Tim. He saw how he glanced often at Jennifer.

"It's safe," said Bruce. "Mostly the geriatric set. Your goons wouldn't be caught dead in here." He pulled open the diner door and they went in.

Tim saw several booths occupied with older people, retirees he surmised. He turned to Bruce. "You weren't lying."

Bruce grinned and guided them to a booth out of earshot from other patrons. After they had placed their orders and the waitress had brought coffee, Bruce looked at Jennifer.

"Guess you saw the news this morning. Looks like your problem might be fixed."

She nodded. "It looked like him, the guy I saw."

"From what I'm told, this Dino Ferrero *was* the guy you saw. Rumor has it, the dude he shot had been stealing secrets and copying files from where he worked and he was found out. It looks like your ex-husband, Robert Downy, told someone in the Cipriano family about it."

"Holy shit," said Tim.

"You...you sure?" said Jennifer staring at Bruce.

Bruce nodded. "Heard something else I haven't verified yet but is interesting."

Jennifer and Tim looked at Bruce who hesitated.

"You gonna tell us or what?" said Tim.

Bruce shifted his gaze to Jennifer. "Seems like your uncle, Roy Wilson, gets his marching orders from high up in the Cipriano family. I haven't figured out who pulls the strings on him, but I'm working on it."

Jennifer listened while shaking her head.

"What's he into?" said Tim.

"Wilson?" Bruce shook his head. "Well, the obvious thing is his real estate developments in Florida and Las Vegas."

"And?" said Tim.

"Word I got, still not verified is that he's part of a multimillion dollar laundry machine. It may be through some of the joints in Las Vegas, since he has quite a few real estate holdings there."

"Is there a connection between Wilson and Downy?" asked Tim.

"I haven't discovered one yet. But my source is kinda scared to tell me much."

"Is anyone...going to come after me?" asked Jennifer hesitantly.

Bruce shook his head. "Don't think so. I believe your uncle took care of it. This guy, Dino, was found in his car down in Waltham. Shot sometime last night."

Jennifer stared at Bruce, and then asked, "My uncle? He did that?"

Bruce shrugged. "Probably a hit by a mob guy, told to clean things up. This way you can't identify anyone."

"They don't fool around," said Tim.

They stopped talking as the waitress delivered their food.

When she walked away Bruce spoke. "Haven't got the Cipriano organization figured out yet. Still working on it." He looked at Jennifer. "I do know that Uncle Roy reports pretty high up the tree. This other guy, Downy, he reports into the organization through some lower branch." He scowled. "I'll have to figure this out."

"So, you think Jennifer is safe; the shooter killed last night?" asked Tim. "That's what you're saying?"

Bruce nodded, chewed and swallowed. "That's what I'm saying. Shooter got taken out last night."

Tim looked at Jennifer. "Your uncle said nothing would happen to you, right? Guess he meant it."

"What's he into?" Jennifer shook her head. "Cipriano?"

"Seems like your uncle and your ex are kinda like rivals," said Bruce. "Maybe even more serious than that after this shooting. I'll be asking around."

"Isn't that dangerous?" she asked.

Bruce shrugged. "It's what I do."

Tim turned to Jennifer. "Bruce is one of the best crime reporters in the Northeast. You wouldn't believe the people who talk to him."

Jennifer grimaced. "Seems dangerous, that's all."

CHAPTER 8

Tim opened a window hoping for a breeze to stir the air as his apartment had been closed for several days.

"This is a nice place, small but nice," said Jennifer as she looked around poking her head in the rooms. "I kinda like it."

"One bedroom is all I need," said Tim. "I have my computer in there and that's where I do most of my work."

Tim went through the stack of mail and tossed most of it in the trash, setting aside bills for attention. A loud knock at the door startled them. Jennifer went to Tim and held onto his arm.

"Who...who is that?" she said in a quivering voice.

"Dunno."

Tim went to the door and looked through the peephole. "Some suits."

There was another knock, louder this time.

Jennifer stood behind Tim as he opened the door against the safety stop.

"Yeah? Help you?" said Tim.

"Tim Beckman?"

Tim nodded. "Yes."

"I'm Agent Nedham and this is Agent Foster, FBI. We're here with Burlington police detective Ed Bryson. We'd like a few minutes of your time."

"What's it about?" Tim didn't open the door. "You have ID?"

Nedham held his ID to the opening at the door. "Just need a few minutes to get your help on something. Would you let us in?"

Tim felt Jennifer's grip tighten. Tim hesitated.

"Only take a few minutes," said Nedham.

Tim removed the safety latch and opened the door. The three men walked into the center of the living room. Nedham and Bryson smiled. Foster didn't.

Tim gestured to the couch. "Have a seat." All three sat down making a tight fit.

Jennifer sat in the wing chair and Tim perched on her armrest.

"As you already know, I'm Tim Beckman. This is Jennifer Wilson."

Tim saw the quick glance Nedham gave Foster who returned an almost imperceptible nod.

"So, what can I do for you?" asked Tim.

Nedham opened a large notebook. Foster took a tape recorder from his jacket pocket and placed it on the coffee table.

Tim shook his head. "What's that for?"

"It's standard procedure. That way there's no misunderstanding," said Foster.

Tim, visibly irritated, glared at them. "Why are you here?"

Foster gave Tim a hard look as he opened his notebook. Neither man offered to reply to Tim's question.

Detective Bryson coughed. "FBI and Burlington police are jointly investigating the incident in the mall the other day."

Nedham smiled at Tim. "Been gone for a couple days?"

Tim shrugged. "Been around."

"We're investigating the shooting of Edward Owens at the Tri-City Mall, as well as the later shooting of Dino Ferrero. Since it involved an employee of an investment company, the FBI elected to participate in the investigation."

Tim hoped Jennifer would keep calm. He responded unenthusiastically. "We heard it on TV."

Nedham nodded. "Suppose so." He then pulled out an 8x10 photograph from his notebook. He laid it flat on the table, and looking at Tim, said, "If you take a look here, one of the cameras in the mall has a pretty good image of you taken about ten minutes before the shooting."

Nedham slid another photo from his notebook. "Here we have you going into Carson's Leather Goods. We identified you from the sales receipt for a leather wallet."

Tim nodded. "Okay. So, what?"

"We're following up with all potential witnesses; see if we can figure out what happened here."

Tim shrugged. "I didn't see anything suspicious."

Nedham frowned. "So where were you when the shooting happened?"

Tim shook his head. "Not sure. I didn't hear any shooting. When I left the leather goods place, I went towards the center of the mall. Picked up a slice of pizza and then I went to the exit."

"Just window shopping?" asked Bryson.

"Sure. Eye-candy everywhere," Tim sniped.

Bryson smiled and shook his head as he leafed through his small notebook.

Nedham pulled out another photo and laid it on the table. "Jennifer, you were nearby the shooting."

Tim got off the armrest and picked up the photo from the table, looked at it, and showed it to Jennifer. She looked into his eyes. Tim nodded.

In a weak voice, Jennifer replied to the question. "I was standing near there. I saw them."

"The shooter and the victim?" asked Nedham.

She nodded, nervously wringing her hands in her lap.

"Did you recognize either man?"

"No."

"You didn't know the victim, Mr. Owens? He worked for Century Design, your ex husband's company when you worked there."

Jennifer shook her head. "I... I didn't recognize him. I was looking at the shooter."

"But you know Mr. Owens, right?" Nedham persisted.

"I knew him when I was working there."

Nedham pulled another photo from his notebook. He held it out and Tim took it.

"Is that the shooter?" asked Nedham.

Tim showed the close-up photo to Jennifer and nodded to her.

"It looks like him."

"You're not certain?"

She shrugged. "Looks like him. His mustache is crooked and I remember seeing that. But, I left there as fast as I could."

Tim handed the photos back to Nedham. "Are we done?"

Foster scowled. "A few more questions."

Nedham looked from Tim to Jennifer. "You folks know Roy Wilson very well?"

"My uncle," said Jennifer.

Nedham waited for more.

"See him on holidays and parties," she added. Then she shrugged. "Never got really close to him."

"Your ex-husband, Robert Downy, does he work for your uncle?" asked Nedham.

Tim kept his hand over Jennifer's clenched fingers. She shook her head. "No. They can't stand each other."

"I see." Nedham coughed. "So, you don't do any work for either of them these days?"

"I'm not working at the moment. I've been applying different places for an Administrative Assistant position."

Nedham turned his attention to Tim. "Your friend, Bruce Engelman... you and he work together? I mean, do you help each other out on projects?"

Tim looked at Nedham, waiting a few seconds before responding. "I don't know what business that is of yours; but no, we are independent. However, we've been friends since college and we talk a lot."

Nedham looked at Jennifer. "Have you ever met Mrs. Owens, maybe at a party?"

Jennifer nodded. "I've seen her a few times, but we never had any conversations."

"What did you think of their relationship? They've been married for some time."

"Nothing jumps out at me. They seemed like any other middle-aged couple."

"When you worked at Century Design, did you get the feeling Mr. Owens was having an affair. Any rumor to that effect?"

Jennifer shook her head. "No. Nothing like that. He was a quiet man."

As Nedham made some notes, Tim stood up. "*Now* are we done? How about we wrap this up?"

Nedham nodded at Foster and the two gathered up their photos, recorder and notebooks.

"We appreciate the time you gave us. It was helpful," said Nedham.

Jennifer stayed seated and Tim went to open the door.

Nedham put out his hand. "Thanks again."

Tim shook hands with both agents and the detective, and then they left. He watched them from behind the Venetian blinds as they walked across the parking lot. Jennifer came up behind him and put her hand on his waist.

"Good riddance," she mumbled.

"They're fishing around for a motive. I gotta admit I'm a bit curious about that myself."

"Owens was just a gentle man. Why...?"

"If it had been just for the briefcase," said Tim, "the guy could've just jammed the gun in Owens's ribs and taken it. Can't see where he had to be killed."

"Could it have been revenge? Or someone worried about something Owens might have seen or heard?"

Tim shrugged. "I suppose so. But why take the briefcase then?"

"Maybe Owens did see something he shouldn't have and he had proof of it in the case."

"Wow. That puts the problem right in Century Design, wouldn't you think?"

Jennifer nodded. "I'm sure if the bastard Downy thought someone was a threat to him, he wouldn't hesitate to kill him."

"What you say... That's about the only thing makes any sense at all," said Tim.

"Those cops were thinking what? That his wife is involved? I don't believe that."

"Not the way it happened," said Tim. "I don't believe it either."

"Cops were sure interested in his wife."

"The cops probably know more than they're letting on. They knew the answers to each question they asked. I guess, in the last few days, you, me and Bruce entered the picture in whatever investigation they're doing," said Tim.

"They're going to make us testify, huh?"

"I don't know," replied Tim.

"My dad told me the RICO guys have been after my uncle for years but never indicted him."

"How about your ex? He must be on their list, too."

Jennifer shook her head. "The less I know about him, the better. Uncle Roy better watch his back. If Downy gets in a jam, I'm sure he'd trade my uncle for FBI favors," said Jennifer.

"Nice guy."

Jennifer pulled on Tim's arm until they both fell onto the sofa. She made herself comfortable, nestling her head against his shoulder, her feet tucked under her.

"I'm kinda glad I met you," she said glancing up at his face.

"I've got to admit, you're growing on me."

"We've known each other less than a week, but I feel comfortable with you."

"Comfortable?" said Tim. "Just comfortable?"

She punched his arm. "You know what I mean."

"I think so."

"You're a good person," she said.

"Just good?"

Again, she punched him.

Tim kissed her head. "I was thinking we should...a..."

She looked up at him, smiling. "I was just thinking the same thing."

CHAPTER 9

Tim's cell phone buzzed. He reached to the end table and picked it up, looked at the display and frowned. "Hello."

"You're delving into something you have no idea about. It's not going to end well for you."

A chill went up Tim's back. "What? Who is this?"

"You got the FBI involved now? You got news reporters involved? You have no idea what you're doing."

"Who the hell is this?"

"Back off, or you'll find out."

The caller hung up.

Jennifer looked at Tim. Her face turned pale. Her lip trembled. "Who... Who was that?"

Tim looked again at the phone display and shook his head. "*Caller Unknown.*"

She grabbed his arm with both hands. "What did they want?"

He looked at her. "It was a warning to back off talking with the FBI and Bruce."

Her look questioned him.

He grimaced. "Somebody's worried about what we're doing; maybe afraid we'll uncover something. It's got to be connected with the mall killing. You think this warning came from some of your uncle's people?"

Jennifer shook her head. "Doubt it. He would have said something. Sounds like something my ex would do. I've heard him on the phone lots of times."

"He's not exactly the high-powered executive type?"

She nodded. "He's high-powered, I guess. But it's in the streets and backrooms of bars. He has lots of guys to do his bidding."

"I thought he was a wheeler-dealer in investments and real estate," said Tim.

"He is, but from what I overheard," said Jennifer, "he's deep into money laundering and different rackets besides his more legitimate businesses. He's done jobs for the Cipriano people."

"You said your uncle doesn't like Downy?"

She shook her head. "He doesn't trust him. Knows he's screwed a lot of people out of a lot of money, some their life savings." She bit her lip. "I learned a lot after I married him."

"If your ex is part of the mall hit, that warning was likely from Downy."

"He scares me," said Jennifer. "If it *was* him, then the warning is for me, too."

"This could get complicated if your uncle had the shooter killed," said Tim.

Tim saw her lower lip tremble.

"I'll never be free of him," she said.

Tim saw a sadness shadow her face.

"He knows I overheard a lot of what he discussed with his people."

"Has he threatened you?" asked Tim.

"Not directly. He didn't have to."

Tim scratched his chin. "Since you can no longer finger the shooter, his attention will be on me. Probably sees *me* as the person to cause him trouble, being a writer and all."

"I don't know." She met his gaze directly. "We had friends, the Engels. We were close with them. They had a house on Cape Cod and took us out on their motor yacht. My ex often went out to their boat and helped Mr. Engels work on it. One day we got a call from the Cape telling us there had been an explosion. Mr. Engels went missing, and the boat burned to the waterline. No one ever heard or saw Mr. Engels again. Engels happened to be a big investor in my ex's Century Design Company."

"Damn," said Tim. "What do you think happened?"

Jennifer shook her head slowly. "I felt so sad for his wife and daughter. They were crushed by it. The police never determined the source of the explosion. Never came up with anything."

"Your ex have anything to say about it?"

"He came home that evening with different clothes than when he left in the morning."

"How did he explain that?"

"He didn't. Said I was mistaken."

"He didn't talk about that day with you?"

"Whenever I asked about it, he seemed eager to dismiss it. Said Engels probably drowned. It didn't really seem to bother him."

"He gain financially from it?"

She nodded. "My dad thinks my ex put a bomb in the boat or had someone do it."

"To gain control of the guy's investment at Century Design?"

"I'm sure."

Tim came back from the kitchen with two beers. "Sorry, it's all I can offer you. I haven't been to the store in a while."

Jennifer smiled. "That's okay. At least it's cold."

"Your ex, he does stuff for the Cipriano people?" asked Tim.

"Lots of stuff. But he's greedy and crazy." Jennifer put down her beer and sat back, leaning into Tim. "Downy set up an investment business before we were married. It always sounded fishy to me. But I kept my mouth shut."

"You mean Century Design?" Tim asked.

"Uh-huh. The business was set up as an LLC and based in Beverly"

Tim frowned. "So, they take people's money and invest it for them?"

Jennifer raised an eyebrow. "His customers are individuals as well as organizations, and other funds."

"How's he attract business?"

"*At this time*, participants are guaranteed a minimum of 7 percent yearly return. Cipriano insists on it. It isn't hard to get investors. Cipriano needs a steady inflow of cash so he can launder his own funds."

Tim shook his head. "How the heck can he *guarantee* 7 percent in today's market, where a good product might pay 4-5 percent?"

Jennifer shook her head. "He told me he *had* to constantly bring in new money."

"Some sort of a Ponzi thing?"

"That's what I think Downy set up initially. But when he got in trouble some years ago, Cipriano basically took over and saved the company from collapse. I understand they established accounts at Century Design to bring in money from Las Vegas that they funnel through some phony Nevada corporation."

"Money laundering?" asked Tim.

Jennifer nodded. "Sounds like it."

"How did he get started? Cipriano money?"

"Not at first. He had the funds invested by the deceased Mr. Engels. And, he enticed a friend of his to partner with him."

"He has a partner?"

"Not any longer. Ron Feldman, who brought a good amount of money into the business, died from heart failure. The LLC had been set up so the survivor would become sole owner if either died. All of a sudden, my dear ex's business was looking up."

Tim raised an eyebrow. "Heart attack?"

"At the hospital, they said he had a diseased heart and suffered kidney failure."

"Really?"

"Well, his wife didn't buy it. She accused my ex of having a hand in his demise."

"What did the police say?" asked Tim.

"I didn't see the coroner's report, but I heard they suspected he had been poisoned."

"They couldn't prove it?"

"They couldn't figure out how the poison had been administered or by whom. The homicide case is still open."

"The cops had to have been suspicious of your ex."

"Feldman died at home, so his wife got first scrutiny by the cops. I'm sure she had nothing to do with it. She and the kids were devastated. After a few days, the cops dropped their suspicions of her and focused instead on my dear old ex."

"Good place to look."

Jennifer shook her head. "The police investigated but were unable to charge him with anything."

"That was the end of it?"

"Not exactly. There was a bank audit scheduled for the month after his partner's death. Those people discovered over a million dollars missing from various investment accounts at Century Design."

Tim's eyes widened. "What happened? Where'd the funds go?"

Jennifer shrugged. "Feldman and my ex were friends since college. I think they conspired to steal from their own company and funnel funds to some foreign account somewhere. I don't have any proof of it, just what little I overheard."

"Did the FBI get involved?"

"A couple agents came by the house. I was still married. They also spent a day or two at Century. I don't think there were charges filed. Not that I heard of."

"How'd he get away with it? Wasn't Cipriano money involved?" asked Tim.

"There was. I think Cipriano paid the restitution to the investors, and now Cipriano is the one that *really* owns the company."

"How did your ex manage to stay alive?"

"He blamed everything on poor Ron Feldman, as he wasn't around to defend himself. I don't know what Feldman and Downy actually did, as no one would tell me anything. Lots of unanswered questions."

"How did your ex avoid going to prison? Didn't the investors sue? And, didn't the FBI have him on fraud?"

Jennifer shrugged. "I don't know how he avoided it, but Cipriano made up all the losses to the investors, and that may have kept him out of prison."

"I would have thought the Cipriano guys would have gotten rid of him."

"Oddly enough, they kept him on. I guess he knew a lot of the business and they didn't."

"He must be on a short leash," said Tim.

"I know Cipriano money is funneled through the phony corporation they set up in Nevada to a bunch of different accounts, all under $10,000, at Century Design. But, besides that, there are many legitimate investment accounts at Century made by individuals and estates. I think they skimmed from everyone."

Tim shook his head. "He's got to be on thin ice."

"When Cipriano bailed him out, they insisted Century Design continue to pay the seven percent on the investment accounts. I understand Cipriano will make up any short fall so the accounts always look good. He has Century working as a money laundering business, and the occasional payments he has to make to keep the accounts current is the 'cost of doing business'."

"And Downy?" Tim asked.

"He'll end up working for them until they put in someone else."

"Someone will find him floating in Boston Harbor when that happens."

CHAPTER 10

Bruce walked into Shorty's, the small neighborhood bar in Woburn. He heard about the place a year ago from a wannabe mobster he helped get a job. The guy had described the place as a popular mob hangout. The late afternoon crowd hadn't arrived yet, only a few tables were occupied. He had the bar seats to himself.

A heavy middle-aged man with *Shorty* stitched on his white T-shirt wiped the bar with a damp towel. He made his way to stand in front of Bruce. "What can I getcha?"

"A cold Bud would be great." He pulled a pen and small notebook from his jacket pocket and flipped to a clean page.

Shorty put the frosty mug on a coaster in front of Bruce and stared at him. "What are ya? Secret Shopper? Or ya writin' a book?"

Bruce grinned. "Freelance, just trying to make a buck. Following up on the murder of Dino Ferrero. I was told he hung out here."

Shorty scowled and pressed hard on the wet towel, wiping where he had wiped only a minute before. "I got nothing to say to you," he mumbled. "Drink your beer and take a hike."

"I'd like to write a little bit of who he was, give him a personality."

"He was a longtime customer, a good guy. That's all I gotta say." Shorty moved away from Bruce, wiping the bar again as he went.

When he turned back, Bruce tried again. "Why do you suppose he was killed? Was he tied in with some bad people?"

Shorty looked past Bruce's shoulder and nodded. "Get lost fella. You're in the wrong place."

Bruce felt a jar to his shoulder as a tall well-dressed man sat down on the stool to his right. Bruce glanced at him in annoyance and turned back to his beer.

"Who's your friend, Shorty?" asked the man.

Shorty placed a shot of whiskey in front of him. "Says he's some kind of reporter. Wants to know about Dino."

The man looked directly at Bruce. "No kidding, a reporter?"

Bruce nodded. "Freelance. Following up on the Dino Ferrero murder. Trying to get something to give him a personality."

"Yeah, like what?" said the man next to him.

"I'm Bruce Engelman. Who are you?"

The man looked at Shorty and grinned. "He wants to know who I am."

"Yeah, he's a scary guy." Shorty smirked. "Maybe ya better tell him before he hurts ya."

The man kept smiling but turned to Bruce. "I'm Bob Downy. That mean anything to you?"

"Not yet."

Shorty snickered. "Some kind of reporter."

Bruce turned to face Downy. "Well, Mister Downy, what can you tell me about Dino Ferrero? Did he work for *you*? Why was he killed?"

Downy tossed the whiskey back and put the shot glass on the bar with some force and then faced Bruce. "Listen, you jerk. Finish your beer and get the hell out of here."

"You can't answer my questions?" asked Bruce.

Downy's face was getting red. "What the hell you know about me, or Dino? You grasping at straws?"

"I was wondering..."

Downy grabbed Bruce's half-finished beer and handed it to Shorty.

"He's done now. He's leaving. Put it on my tab." Downy was on his feet, a tight grip on Bruce's arm, forcing him towards the door. He pushed the door open and shoved Bruce into the daylight. "Don't come back."

Bruce threw his hands in the air. "Yeah, whatever."

Bruce headed home in the rush hour traffic. He realized he hadn't learned much at Shorty's. "I've been tossed out of better places," he mumbled. But, he was certain of a tight connection between Dino Ferrero and Bob Downy. Then, he changed his mind and headed to Chelmsford. There, he pulled into the Dunkin' Donuts parking lot and opened his cell phone.

"Hey Tim, Bruce here."

"Yeah, I know. What's up?"

"I'm stopping at Leon's Diner for supper. Want to join me?"

"You buying?"

"No. I'm low on funds."

"Leon's. Yeah, I can tell."

"Well, you coming or what?"

"Okay if I bring Jennifer?"

"Sure. She's gorgeous."

"Be there in thirty."

Jennifer put her arm through Tim's as they walked from the car to the diner entrance. "Is this the best he can do?" she asked.

"Says he's low on funds."

"Why did he want us here? Why not just talk on the phone?"

"I guess we'll find out." Tim pulled open the door and spotted Bruce in a booth at the far end of the diner.

Bruce looked up from a notebook and smiled, his gaze lingering on Jennifer. "Glad you could make it. I didn't want to talk on the phone."

"Why not?" asked Jennifer.

"Paranoid maybe." He raised an eyebrow. "I got a one-on-one with your ex today."

Jennifer just stared.

"How'd you manage that?" asked Tim. "Might be unhealthy."

A waitress approached and they ordered food. Tim asked for the blue-plate special, the meatloaf platter. Jennifer wrinkled her nose at that and ordered a seafood salad. Bruce stayed with his steady diet of hamburgers. Tim asked for coffee. Jennifer and Bruce asked for a diet soda.

Jennifer looked at Tim. "Meatloaf?"

"I like meatloaf." Tim shrugged. "How bad can it be?"

"I've had it," said Bruce. "Comes with good gravy."

Jennifer shook her head. "You guys..."

"So, what've you got to say for yourself?" asked Tim, looking at Bruce.

"It's public information that the shooter at the mall was Dino Ferrero. So, I checked with some of my unsavory sources and was told that Dino hung out at a bar called Shorty's."

"Where's that?" asked Tim.

"It's a little dive in Woburn," Bruce replied. "Anyhow, I went down there and laid it on that I was a reporter and started asking for background on Dino." Bruce looked at Tim then Jennifer. "You know, get some info to give him a human face in an article I'm writing."

Tim rolled his eyes. "Of course. How did that approach work out?"

Bruce scowled. "Not so good. Bar tender, this Shorty guy, wouldn't give me the time of day. He told me to drink up and take a hike."

Tim shook his head. "Maybe you should've."

"I must've ticked him off, for then this guy shows up from behind me and starts quizzing me. Said he was Bob Downy. I pretended I'd never heard of him."

Jennifer stared with her mouth open.

"What'd he say?" asked Tim.

"I started in on him asking for some personal info on Dino, saying I wanted to write an article. But he wasn't going to tell me anything, wanted me out of there. I asked who might have killed Dino."

"Holy crap," gasped Tim.

"Yeah, well, next thing happened was him hustling me out the door."

"So, what did you do?" asked Tim.

"Out in the car, I searched the Internet and saw where Downy is listed as a partner in Century Design. He's also listed as a partner in another business called Ocean Tower in Salem. It's another investment company dealing in commercial real estate."

"Yeah, but what did you come away with at Shorty's?" asked Tim. "You must've got a feel of something."

"I got the feeling that Shorty and Downy weren't happy that Dino had been killed. But Downy wasn't about to say anything or point a finger at anyone."

"Who...who *did* kill him?" asked Jennifer.

Bruce looked at her. "It's looking more and more that it was your uncle or someone that owed him one."

Tim turned to Jennifer. "Your uncle did say he would take care of the problem."

CHAPTER 11

Shorty placed drinks in front of the two men. It was early afternoon and no other customers were in the place. He knew enough not to linger and retreated quickly behind the bar.

Robert Downy took a sip of bourbon and looked at his companion. "Well, what are we going to do?"

Angelo Costello shook his head. "There's got to be two more CDs somewhere."

Downy scowled. "No shit, that's brilliant."

Angelo put down his beer mug. "Damn it, there are only two possibilities. This guy, Owens, has two more CDs in the deposit box or he's given them to someone."

"I called the widow yesterday," said Downy. "She claims the cops took away Owens's computer, a stack of CDs and some files. She says there's nothing left in his desk."

"You believe her?" asked Angelo.

Downy nodded slowly. "Yeah… Pretty sure she's telling me the truth."

"Unless she holds *you* responsible; then she might hold back."

"Yeah, I hear you. But I didn't get any hint she blames me," said Downy.

"Hate to say this, but that still leaves your ex wife in the picture."

Downy took a sip from his drink and then stared at the glass for a moment. "It *is* suspicious, but hard for me to believe, knowing her."

"She's bound to know a lot about you and the company. Don't you think?" said Angelo.

It was a few seconds before Downy responded. "Yeah."

"She was right there when Owens entered the mall. Right near the bank."

Downy nodded. "I need to get those two CDs before the cops get their hands on them. I hate to think what may be on them."

"You didn't have any suspicion of this Owens guy? Christ, he worked for you since the beginning."

Downy shook his head slowly. "He was always so intense and quiet and a damn good accountant."

"Cipriano is gonna want to know what his exposure might be. What'll I tell him?"

Downy glared at Angelo.

Angelo squirmed in his seat. "Damn it, if I don't tell him stuff...and he finds out somewhere else...it's my ass."

"So, what're you really saying?"

"He'll want this tidied up right away."

"*Tidied up*? You mean like kill her?" Downy shook his head.

Angelo scowled. "You know what he'll say."

"I don't want her dead, goddamn it." Downy glared at Angelo. "The police will automatically focus on me, ex husband, and I don't need that."

"It's either she has them or we find out the CDs are in the bank vault – or somewhere else." Angelo paused for a second. "If they're in the bank, chances are the cops already have them."

"How soon will you know?" asked Downy. "*You* got *those* connections."

Angelo shrugged. "Hard to say. Maybe a week. There's a woman on the inside..."

"Yeah, so I have a few days?"

"Yes. But the boss will want something done if it's not in the bank vault."

"I'll work on it. You let me know as soon as you hear, okay?"

Angelo nodded.

—

Robert Downy sat in his office at Century Design waiting to hear from two men he had dispatched a couple days earlier on an important task. His phone buzzed and he pressed the flashing button.

"Bob, I have Art Morrison and Nick Caruso here. Are you expecting them?"

"Thank you, Becky. Please bring them up."

When the receptionist brought the two men to his doorway, he waved them in. "Close the door and have a seat."

Downy looked at Caruso, the smarter and more experienced of the two. "Nick, how'd it go?"

Nick leaned forward in his chair. His eyes darted around the room.

"No one can hear us in here," said Downy.

"Well, okay," said Nick with a shrug. "We went to the chick's place first and did a thorough search. It's a small apartment and didn't take us long. Art looked at her computer while I looked through her papers. I found her bank statements and receipts, but there was no mention of a safe deposit box. I didn't see any receipt for a postal box either."

"Was there anything with Century Design on it? Letters, copies of anything?" asked Downy.

"Nick and Art shook their heads in unison. "Nothing," said Art. "Nothing in her computer either."

"You tailed her?" asked Downy.

"We didn't see her either day," said Nick. "She never showed up at her place."

Downy frowned and they were silent for a moment.

Nick started again. "We took a look at the guy's place. Beckman."

"What'd you find?"

"Not a damn thing. His apartment is small and pretty sparsely furnished. He had all his financial stuff and legal papers in one dresser drawer. We went through everything and didn't find a thing. He had a few CDs by his computer, but they were just programs. The computer booted up right away, and Art checked out the hard drive but didn't see anything you'd be interested in."

"You didn't see him either?" asked Downy.

Art shook his head. "We went back to the chick's place but didn't see either one."

"No sign of them, so we went to this other apartment."

"Bruce Engelman?"

"Yeah." Nick shook his head. "What a dump. Crap piled up everywhere. Must've been a hundred CDs in a stack that we looked through. The damn computer had a password to get into it, so forget that."

"Looked through his papers and desk? Anything there?" asked Downy, scowling.

"We tore the place apart. There wasn't any key or receipt or paperwork for a bank deposit box or postal box. No papers about Century Design. Nothing."

Downy turned to look out the window. His lips were clamped tight. Then he shook his head and turned back to the two men. Pulling open a desk drawer, he took out a clip of money. He tossed it to Nick. "It's what we agreed on. Thanks for doing the job."

"Wish we had better news for you," said Nick.

Downy nodded and pushed a button on his desk phone. "Becky, the gentlemen are leaving."

"Be right there," came the reply.

The two men stood up. "You need anything else, we're around," said Nick.

There was a knock and the door opened. "Becky will see you out," said Downy.

When the door closed again, Downy turned toward the window and stared into the distance. Tomorrow was the funeral for Edward Owens. He would have to go, maybe say a few words. The widow, Elaine, would be there, and he would have to publicly reassure her of his support. Later, he could do it in private. He wondered if she harbored lingering suspicion for the hit on Owens. He had called Elaine as soon as the news came on the TV. She *seemed* to still have faith in him, but was confused and saddened as to why anyone would want to kill her husband. The police would be a different story; he expected there would be a detective or two in the crowd looking at him and the widow. Hopefully, the day would pass quietly.

CHAPTER 12

Bruce, Tim and Jennifer met again at Leon's Diner. This time only Bruce ordered food. He looked at his friends, and grinned. "All our places have been tossed. Gives you the idea they're looking for something."

"Ha-ha." Tim scowled. "Be better if we knew who did it."

"And why," added Jennifer.

Bruce shook his head. "What are they looking for? That's what's important."

"It's got to be something they think all three of us might've had access to," said Jennifer. "But what?"

"I think its Jennifer who's at risk here," said Tim. "They're looking at Bruce and me only because we're with her."

"It makes me wonder," replied Bruce. "Do the bad guys think Jennifer was at the shooting site by coincidence, or not?"

"Why? What are you getting at?" asked Tim.

"Well, from the mall video pictures they showed on TV, it's apparent the dead guy, Edward Owens, was carrying a briefcase into the mall. There's been no mention of it on any news program. I haven't seen any other pictures, but I'd be willing to wager that the shooter grabbed it. I don't want to conclude that was why Owens was killed, but since the shooter is now dead, someone else surely has it."

The three were silent for a moment.

"And this is why they tossed our places?" asked Jennifer. "There was something in the briefcase that prompted this?" She shook her head. "I don't understand."

Bruce looked from Tim to Jennifer. "Maybe they found something in the case that suggested Owens was going to meet you – give you something."

"Damn it. I wasn't there to meet him – or anyone else!"

"What would give those guys that idea?" asked Tim.

"They might've found something that *suggests* someone has something important related to Century Design." said Bruce.

Jennifer shook her head. "I don't have anything from Downy's work, not a single damn thing."

"You didn't know Edward Owens?" asked Bruce.

"He worked at Century when I did, but I didn't really *know* him. I didn't report to him, I was just a clerk. I saw him and his wife at one of Downy's parties. This was a couple years ago. We were introduced."

"Those guys must think that you have or were given something that would be bad for them," said Tim.

"They must know by now that none of us has what they're looking for," said Bruce. "And yet, they are still looking for it, what ever *it* is."

Suddenly Jennifer sat up and looked from Bruce to Tim. "I don't know that Mrs. Owens would remember me, but I could go visit her and ask if there is anything in her husband's stuff that would help in discovering who killed him."

"She would talk to you?" asked Tim.

"I don't know." Jennifer shrugged. "I don't know why she wouldn't."

"Unless she's involved," said Bruce.

Jennifer shook her head. "I don't believe that. Why?"

"Well then, she's got to have her own suspicions, even if she didn't tell them to the police," suggested Tim.

"If I can get her to talk about it, she might let me look at his stuff – see if I can find out who's coming after me, and why." Her eyes filled. "I just can't live like this."

Tim put his hand on hers. "We'll figure it out." He looked at Bruce. "Won't we?"

Bruce nodded. "Yep. Going to see Mrs. Owens sounds like a good idea – if she'll see you."

Tim drove Jennifer into Lexington the next day, and looking at the GPS display, found Mrs. Owens' street. He stopped the car so that it would be mostly shielded from view from anyone in the house.

"I'll wait for you here," said Tim. "Don't need to intimidate her by having me with you."

"Okay, but keep your cell phone on." Jennifer kissed him on the cheek and left the car.

Jennifer heard the chimes from deep in the house when she pressed the doorbell. It was ten seconds before she heard the bolt being pulled back. Then the door opened. An impeccably dressed middle-aged woman appraised her, and then smiled.

"Yes? May I help you?"

"Mrs. Owens?"

"Yes."

"My name is Jennifer Wilson. I'm the ex-wife of Robert Downy, the man that owns Century Design and the man your husband worked for. I was hoping you would give me a few minutes."

The scowl on Mrs. Owens's face didn't give Jennifer much hope. "Then you must know about my husband. I really don't have anything to say."

"I am very sorry for your loss. It...it was quite a shock."

"Shock? Yes. What is it you wish to talk to me about?"

Jennifer saw the tenseness drain from the woman as she took a step back, opening the door wider.

"Come in. Maybe a few minutes."

"Thank you, Mrs. Owens."

Jennifer followed the woman into a well-appointed living room.

"Please. Have a seat." She pointed to the sofa.

Jennifer sat down, placing her purse next to her thigh. "You have a beautiful house."

"Thank you. Now, what is it you wish to talk about? You have to understand, I'm not very fond of the company my husband worked for." She dropped her gaze to her lap, intertwining her fingers.

"I understand. I also have some thoughts about the company and my ex-husband that I haven't said out loud."

Mrs. Owens peered at her over the top of her glasses. "Oh? Does it have to do with my husband?"

"I met your husband at Century Design several years ago, but I really don't know him. You probably don't recall, but I was introduced to you and your husband a couple years back at one of Downy's parties."

Mrs. Owens shook her head. "No."

"I was horrified at what happened to him." Jennifer paused and bit her lip. "I was in the mall at the time and saw it."

Mrs. Owens's eyes widened, her mouth dropped open. "You...you were there?"

Jennifer nodded. "I came out of the bank and was heading back to the main entrance when I saw something out of the corner of my eye. I guess it was the odd movement. A man had stumbled, actually falling, when I saw another man trying to hold him up. It was a face I had seen before."

"My Edward?" gasped Mrs. Owens.

"It was. But it's the other man I recognized."

"What...what happened?"

"This other man was holding your husband up from falling and sat him down against the wall. I didn't hear what he said to a passerby, but that fellow kept on walking, seemingly unperturbed."

"Didn't someone call for help?" Elaine stared, her face ashen.

"The man with your husband had a cell phone out. Maybe he called."

"Who...who was this man? Did he...did he hurt my husband? Is he the one...?"

"Mrs. Owens, I'm sorry...I didn't see if he did...just saw him help your husband sit against the wall. Then he grabbed your husband's briefcase. That's when he looked at me. I guess I must have been staring. I'm sorry, I should've called 9-1-1, but then I saw him staring at me and I got scared."

"Who...who was he?"

"I recognized him, although I don't know his name. I think he realized I recognized him and started to follow me up the corridor. I was getting really frightened and started to run. I got outside before he could catch up to me and a nice man helped me escape."

Mrs. Owens was shaking her head. Jennifer saw her bite down on her lip and wring her hands. "But why?" She looked at Jennifer with tear filled eyes. "Why would someone kill him?"

"I don't know. I think the man that attacked your husband walked away with the briefcase he was carrying."

"He...he was going to the bank?" Mrs. Owens pulled a tissue from her pocket and wiped her nose.

"What was in the briefcase?"

Mrs. Owens shook her head. "I don't know. Company stuff, I guess." She looked at Jennifer. "My God, was he killed for that...for the briefcase?"

Jennifer shook her head and shrugged. "I...I'm sorry."

Neither woman spoke for a minute. Mrs. Owens wiped her eyes with the tissue.

Jennifer leaned forward and spoke softly. "Would you let me look through his desk, see if there is anything that would shed light on what happened?"

Mrs. Owens stared at her husband's desk, now piled up with books and cartons. "The police came here with a warrant. They took the computer and some files and CDs. There isn't much left but junk. It's all piled up on top. I haven't had the energy to go through it. You may if you wish." She stood up. "While you do that, I'll go make us some tea. You drink tea?"

Jennifer stood and smiled. "Yes. Thank you."

When Mrs. Owens left the room, Jennifer busied herself at the desk. She quickly went through the contents of the cartons, setting them aside as uninteresting. She moved books on IRS regulations and tax preparation to the edge of the desk. *I won't find anything here, not if the cops did a good job.* She wondered how long the woman would be in the kitchen, and then rifled through the desk drawers. *Someone picked these clean.* Disappointed, she put her hands on the edge of the desk, the heavy leather writing-pad under her fingers. She looked at it, admiring the tooled leather and padded side pockets. On impulse, she lifted the edge closest to her by several inches. Hidden underneath were two CDs.

Her heart seemed to skip a beat as she pulled them out from under the heavy pad and slipped them quickly into her purse. She let the pad drop and started to return the objects from where she had pushed them, back onto the writing pad. When she heard footsteps, Jennifer stood up, her purse under her arm, her heart racing.

Mrs. Owens glanced quickly around the room before setting the tea service on an antique table in front of the sofa. "Well, did you find anything useful?"

"No. The cops sure didn't leave much. Mostly just tax stuff," said Jennifer.

The two women sat on the sofa and started on their tea.

"I don't know why this happened to my Edward." Mrs. Owens looked at Jennifer. "Was he killed for the briefcase? Why?"

"Maybe someone thought he had something very valuable...or very important," offered Jennifer.

"He was ready to retire. Now this…"

Jennifer noticed she was biting her lip. *Is she trying not to cry? Poor woman lost her husband. She is so much younger than he, isn't she? She's maybe 40, and he was ready to retire?*

"Was he retiring early?" asked Jennifer.

"He was going on 62 and wanted to retire while he could enjoy it."

"I'm sorry…"

Mrs. Owens nodded and put her cup down on the saucer. Jennifer sensed that she should leave and stood up.

"Thank you for your hospitality. I'm sorry it had to be on such a sad occasion," said Jennifer.

Mrs. Owens smiled. "I'll see you out."

Jennifer closed the car door and took a deep breath, hoping her heart would slow down.

Tim started the car. "Did you find out anything? I was getting worried."

When the car moved past some shrubbery, Jennifer glanced back at the house and noticed two slats of the Venetian blinds were separated. *She's looking at me.* "Maybe."

"I called Bruce. He'll meet us at the Dunkin' Donuts in Chelmsford," said Tim.

Jennifer nodded. "She *seemed* distraught about her husband. Didn't look like fake tears."

"I'm surprised she even let you in the house. What did she tell you?"

"She actually let me look through his desk."

"Wow. Smooth talker, you are."

"Of course, the police had already taken the computer and other stuff. She said there wasn't anything on the desk of any use, but I asked to look anyway and she said okay."

Tim looked at her for a moment. "You didn't believe her?"

Jennifer shrugged. "I don't know. I was hopeful there'd be a clue."

"Did you find something?" asked Tim.

Jennifer smiled. "I found two CDs under the leather writing-pad. I have them."

"What? You just took them?"

"Slipped them into my purse."

"Really? Wow. Maybe we'll get lucky."

They pulled into the parking lot at Dunkin' Donuts.

"I'll run in and get some goodies. Bruce will be along soon," said Tim.

Tom purchased coffee and a box of Munchkins and got back in the car. Jennifer described her experience in the Owens house as they sipped their coffee. A few minutes later there was a knock on the driver's window. Tim motioned for Bruce to get in the rear seat.

"We got you a coffee and some Munchkins," said Tim as he passed the food back to Bruce.

"You guys are okay," said Bruce. "So, Jennifer, what happened?" Bruce looked expectantly at her. "Did you get to talk to her?"

"I did," grinned Jennifer. "She even served tea."

"Tea? I'm surprised she even talked to you."

"I told her I was the ex-wife of Robert Downy, the man that owns Century Design. I asked her for a few minutes of her time. She made it sound like she wasn't real fond of Century Design."

"No surprise there," said Bruce.

"She appeared distraught," commented Jennifer, "but hard to tell."

"What did you two talk about?" asked Bruce.

"She said she didn't understand why anyone would kill her husband. It finally came down to the briefcase he was carrying; that maybe there was something valuable in it and someone knew about it."

"Did she sound sincere?" asked Bruce.

Jennifer nodded. "I asked if I could look around the stuff in his desk. She hesitated but then agreed. However, she said that the police had been there with a warrant and had carried off the computer and his files and most anything of importance. I asked if I could look and see if there was anything that would shed light on why he was killed. She accepted that and went to make tea while I poked around on his desk."

"She actually made tea?" asked Bruce.

Jennifer nodded. "Yep. She was gone for several minutes, while I quickly went through the desk and the stuff on top of it. Just before she returned with the tea set, I accidentally discovered two CDs lying under the big leather writing-pad. I slipped them into my purse just a few seconds before she returned."

Jennifer handed Bruce the two CDs. "I guess the cops missed them."

Bruce looked at her with a large grin. "Nancy Drew, lead detective."

"I was surprised the cops or someone hadn't found them. But they're so thin, it didn't perturb the heavy leather writing surface," said Jennifer.

"Is there any marking on them?" asked Tim.

"There's only a number 2 marked on this one," said Bruce. He looked at the second CD. "This other has a 1 marked on it. Nothing else. My laptop is in my car; I'll get it and see if we can read what's on these." He moved to open the door.

"Then what?" said Tim. "What do we do with them?"

"Let's wait and see what's on them before worrying about it," said Bruce getting out of the car.

Tim and Jennifer turned around in their seats to face Bruce as he booted up his laptop.

"Okay. Let's take a look at them." Bruce inserted the CD marked as "1" into the computer CD slot.

"What's on it?" asked Jennifer anxiously. "What do you see?"

"I'm looking. Gimme a minute," replied Bruce. "There are several PowerPoint organization charts," said Bruce as he poked more keys. "We got some flow charts that show routing of different funds."

"Really? Let's see," exclaimed Tim.

Bruce turned the laptop to let Tim and Jennifer see the file listings. "This CD doesn't have anything else on it; just a lot of charts. Let's look at the other one." Bruce removed CD number 1 and installed the one marked "2."

Looking at the file index, Bruce grunted and poked some keys. "Here's a spreadsheet with fund names, dollar amounts and people's names." He looked up at Jennifer and Tim. "This could be very interesting."

"What else is on there?" asked Tim.

"There are lots of separate work sheets linked into this spreadsheet. And lots of other spreadsheets."

Jennifer looked at Tim. "You think Owens was killed for these CDs?"

"It looks like the killer was hoping to get these, number 1 and 2, as well as others that may have been in the briefcase."

"If he even knew that any CDs existed," said Bruce. "We don't know that."

"We gotta figure out why Owens was really killed," said Jennifer. "Don't we?"

Tim and Bruce both looked at her and nodded.

"I gotta think getting a hold of these CDs will be paramount for Downy and the mob guys he's associated with," said Bruce. Then he added, "If he knows about them."

"How're we going to protect them?" asked Tim.

Bruce took a thumb drive from within his computer bag and inserted it into the computer USB port. "I'll make a copy of these CDs on this thumb drive. It's easy to hide." He looked at Jennifer. "Meantime, you need to find a really good hiding place for these CDs."

Bruce removed the CD from his computer and handed both to Jennifer. "None of us can have a copy of these CDs on our own computer. If someone comes looking for the CDs, we don't want them to know we saw what is on them." He looked at Jennifer. "Do you think you could find a hiding place that would be secure?"

Jennifer glanced at Tim, and then nodded. "I'll find a place."

CHAPTER 13

The light was blinking on Robert Downy's phone.

"Yes, Diane."

"There is an Elaine Owens on the phone. Are you in today?"

Downy smiled. "Sure. I'll talk to Elaine."

When the line was connected, Downy greeted her. "Hello Elaine. I was thinking about you."

"Oh Bob, were you?"

"I was hoping we could get away for awhile soon."

"I'd like that, but I'm calling because something odd happened yesterday," said Elaine.

The happiness went out of Downy's voice. "Odd? How?"

"A young lady came to the house yesterday afternoon, Jennifer Wilson."

A chill came over Bob. "Jennifer...? My ex wife?"

"Yes. She came in a car with a man driving. I couldn't tell who it was."

Bob gulped. "What did she want?"

"She said she had been the woman in the mall and had *seen* the shooting. I told her how devastated I was about it. I said I didn't understand why anyone would want to kill my Edward."

"Uh-huh," said Downy. "What did she want from you?"

"She said she saw my husband with this man who propped him against the wall. I don't know who called 9-1-1, but she said this man grabbed Edward's briefcase and was set to leave when he spotted her looking at him."

"Wow. Really?"

"She said she recognized the shooter but didn't know his name." Elaine caught her breath and continued. "She said the shooter saw her, realized what she had seen, and started to follow her. But before he could catch up to her, some man joined her just outside."

"Jesus. What did Jennifer want?"

"She said she wanted to get to the bottom of it, find out who killed Edward. She seemed disturbed by it. Then she asked if she could look around his desk for clues."

"You serious?"

"I told her the police had already taken the computer and a box full of files. She asked to look anyway, and I didn't want to seem suspicious, so I let her rummage through the desk. She didn't find anything."

"I don't like this, Elaine. What the heck is she up to? Is she working with somebody?"

"She didn't find anything. I'm not sure what she really wanted. She must have known the police would've already taken everything."

"She didn't suggest anything about *us*, did she?"

"No. And I wouldn't have let her go there."

"I'll have to investigate what she's up to. Hopefully she's playing amateur detective and isn't working with someone."

"What should I do?"

"Have the police given you a list, yet, of what they found in the safe deposit?"

"A detective brought it by last evening," replied Elaine.

"Would you read it to me?"

"Sure. I have it right here." Elaine read off the items listed as the contents of the safe deposit box. It included financial records, a passport and $46,000 in cash. There were no CDs and no notebooks.

"When will you get the items back?"

"Detective didn't know."

"Turns out, the briefcase *eventually* ended up with some people I know. Lets leave it at that. They found two numbered CDs in it, leading these folks to believe there are at least two others. These guys really want to find them as they could expose them to trouble."

"Cipriano?"

"Yes."

"But why kill my Edward? He was a good man."

"I don't know. It looked to me like a botched robbery."

"I don't like those people you know. They're animals."

"The guy I talked to said the information on the two CDs he saw was very descriptive to the operation of Century Design. He was worried that the two missing CDs might detail the Cipriano involvement with Century. Actually, the FBI getting hands on this kind of information could bring us *all* real trouble."

"But what can *I* do?"

"Nothing. Let me worry about it. In the meantime, we can't be talking about this stuff anymore on the phone. Don't want anyone picking up on it."

"Okay. But God, I miss seeing you."

"Me too. But we have to let some time go by," said Downy. "Then we'll plan a way to retire in Belize."

"Oh Bob, I want that so much."

"Me too. Gotta run. Love you." Downy hung up.

Bob Downy wondered if his office phone might be tapped. He'd have to get the security service back in and test the lines and look for bugs. He had been told there was a box that could be set on his desk that would tell him when it detected a bug on the line. Those service guys were costing him a fortune, but worth it, he decided. There was less chance of being overheard on his cell phone, though no guarantee there either.

He pulled his cell phone from his jacket pocket and pressed the speed dial for Antonio Cipriano.

"Tony."

"Downy here."

"You have some good news?"

"There are no CDs or notebooks listed on the police inventory of the safe deposit box."

"How do you know?"

"She read me the list."

"What *was* in it?"

"Mainly a passport and $46,000 in cash."

"He was getting ready to go somewhere?" asked Cipriano. "You giving him a long vacation?"

"Hardly. I have no idea where he got all that money or what it was for. I never got a hint that he was planning a vacation…not until I intercepted his phone call with some travel agent. Then, I got really worried as to what he was up to. At the time I was more worried about what he might be taking to the feds. I had to get the briefcase and see what he was taking out of the office."

"He probably wouldn't tell you, if he was skimming. Would he?"

"Damn, he was such a milquetoast kind of guy."

"Yeah, they're the ones you gotta watch."

"Looks like he might have been in the mall to get his stuff and flee the country," said Downy.

"And his wife, she doesn't know a damn thing?"

"I've talked to her. I don't believe she had any idea what he was up to. His plans, whatever they were, might not have included her."

"Owens could have been at the bank to remove his cash and passport. But, then what would he have done with the two CDs? Would he put them together with CD number 1 and 2? And, where the hell are *they?*"

"CDs number 1 and 2 could be very harmful to us," said Downy. "The ones we have are serious enough."

"I gotta wonder, was Owens working with the FBI, and do they have the first two CDs? Or did the bastard hide them someplace in his house? Or did he trust them with someone else, your fuckin' ex for instance?"

"If the FBI had them, we would have heard from them in some way by now. Don't you think?"

"Maybe. How are we gonna find them?"

"We searched my niece's place and her boyfriend's place, and I have been in Owens's house looking around, but nothing's turned up."

"We gotta find them. What about your ex wife?"

"Owens barely knew my ex wife. There's no reason he would have confided in her."

"I'm not convinced. I want you to do a more thorough job on her and her friends. I want those CDs. You hearing me on this?"

Downy heard the threat clearly. "Okay Tony. I'm on it."

"Good."

"I've got a question I have to ask you," said Downy. "Why was Dino Ferrero hit? He was a valuable asset to me."

"He was a bungling idiot. Didn't do what he was told. If the DA got him on the witness stand, he'd cause us a lot of grief."

"Is it because he saw my ex wife in the mall and she saw him? Did Roy Wilson have a hand in this?" asked Downy.

"Let go of this. I don't want to have to tell you again. You need to spend your time worrying about those missing CDs. Frankly, if they aren't recovered soon, the boss might want to protect himself..."

"I hear you."

Cipriano hung up.

Bob Downy rang the doorbell and waited. Just as he was about to ring again, Elaine Owens opened the door.

"Hi Elaine."

"Oh Bob, it's so good to see you. Please, come in."

Elaine pushed the door closed when Bob entered and leaned into him as his arms encircled her.

He broke away from a passionate kiss and shook his head.

Elaine frowned. "What's wrong?"

"I'm sorry. They're really leaning on me to find some damn CDs that they claim Edward had. I guess if they land in the hands of the cops, it could prove more than embarrassing for them. Actually, it wouldn't be good for us either."

"Cipriano?"

Bob nodded. "He insists that I find them. So, we have to do a really thorough search here – from top to bottom."

"I'll help you." Elaine grimaced. "Actually, I hoped we could spend some time alone, like we used to."

Bob pulled her against him and kissed her. "Me too. Some day we'll leave all this behind."

"Let's look for those CDs. How do you want to do this?"

"The cops listed thirty-two CDs they confiscated here. None were the ones we're looking for."

"I've accounted for every CD they took," said Elaine. "There weren't any labeled number 1 or number 2."

"Edward may not have brought them home," said Bob. "That's a real possibility."

Elaine nodded. "Okay."

"We'll start upstairs and work our way to the basement. I'll take a look in the attic. You could start in the main bedroom. When we're done, I'll finish up in the garage."

"Okay. It'll take us some time."

"I'm sorry, Elaine. We just have to do this."

"Maybe afterward…?"

CHAPTER 14

Tim drove Jennifer to a meeting the FBI had requested at their office in Burlington, MA. He parked the Chevy Malibu in the visitor parking area.

He looked at his watch. "You have about ten minutes before your appointment."

"I hate this." She looked at Tim. "I'm scared. They want to talk to me *alone.*"

Tim put his hand on her shoulder. "You haven't done anything wrong. You're probably the only witness they have."

"Suppose they try to intimidate me...try to make me say something stupid?"

"You're not under arrest. You can get up and walk out. It's your right."

"They probably know I was in the Owens home, talking with the wife. I bet they spotted me."

"It'll be okay. They might've had a stakeout at her house. That could be expected."

Jennifer looked at her watch. "I better get in there."

Tim kissed her. "You'll be okay."

She smiled and left the car.

Special Agent Brian Ludlow guided Jennifer into a meeting room. The Spartan interior had a table and four chairs. Two men stood as Jennifer entered.

"Jennifer, this is Agent Steve Murdoch, pointing to his left, and Agent Walter Barrow."

The men smiled and said their greeting before sitting back down. Agent Ludlow placed a voice recorder on the table. He looked at Jennifer.

"We record all meetings as standard practice," as he pointed to two cameras on the wall near the ceiling. "We use *this* recorder to make sure we don't miss anything."

Agent Ludlow introduced the participants to the recorder and gave the date and time. "My main focus is going to be Jennifer's recollection of her meeting with Elaine Owens."

He looked at Jennifer. "Let's start with why you went to see Mrs. Owens."

Jennifer looked at the men present and then turned back to Ludlow. "Seeing the man get killed like that; well, it affected me. It was terrible. I wanted to know why Mr. Owens had been killed. It ate at me."

"So, you went to see his wife?" asked Ludlow.

"Uh-huh. I went to see her about what her husband's mission at the mall might've been and who might want him dead."

"You didn't come forward to the police at the time. Now you're playing detective?"

"I was scared to come forward then. The shooter had seen me. I ran out of the mall and I asked a man to help me get away from there."

Ludlow looked at his notes. "That would be Timothy Beckman."

Jennifer nodded. "Tim, yes."

"You and he...what? Now friends?"

"Yes."

"I'm perplexed. You decided to go to Mrs. Owens's home and ask questions about her husband?" Ludlow shook his head. "Isn't that a bit bold?"

Jennifer shrugged. "Guess so."

"Even more surprising...she let you in."

"I was hoping she would."

"How did the conversation go?"

"Okay, I guess. I told her I had seen her husband get shot. She seemed very keen to hear more about it. I told her what I saw, and said I wanted to find out who killed her husband, and maybe see if he couldn't be brought to justice."

"It's a wonder she didn't call the police."

"She seemed saddened by her husband's murder and wondered out loud who could have done it and why."

"She offered an opinion?" asked Ludlow.

Jennifer shook her head. "She said she didn't know he had enemies."

"Then what?"

"She went to make tea."

The agent next to Ludlow rolled his eyes.

"I had asked if I could look through the stuff on her husband's desk in the meantime. She said I could, but that the police had already been there with a warrant and had taken away most things."

"What did you find? Anything to further your *investigation?*" asked Ludlow.

"No. Mostly receipts and billing statements. I guess the police really did take everything."

Ludlow made some notes and then looked at Jennifer. "Let's go back to the shooter. Did you recognize him?"

"I thought I had seen him at one of my uncle's parties."

"And this guy's name was Dino Ferrero, right?"

"I recognized him when they showed his face on TV, but I didn't know his name."

"Right. You had seen him at your uncle's place. When was this?"

"Last fall. Maybe September."

"We're talking about Roy Wilson, aren't we?"

Jennifer nodded. "My uncle."

"Did *you* have anything to do, either directly or indirectly, with the demise of Mr. Ferrero?"

Jennifer shook her head. "No. Of course not."

"It's a rather lucky event though, isn't it?"

"Huh?"

"I mean it got rid of any threat from being a witness."

"I have no knowledge of why he died or who would have done it," said Jennifer.

"Do you know if your ex husband and uncle have done business with the Cipriano organized crime organization?"

Jennifer pursed her lips. "Over the years there have been whispered rumors, but I have no direct knowledge of this."

Ludlow looked at his notes and added a few more. "Let's go back to Mrs. Owens."

Jennifer shrugged and resettled herself on the chair.

"Did Mrs. Owens seem truthful to you, or deceitful?"

"I didn't think she was lying. Why would she?"

"Mrs. Owens worked at Century Design for the past year until about three months ago. Did you know that?"

"I think she was a book keeper."

"Did you know *Mr.* Owens well enough to have any conversations with him?"

"I had seen him at Century, but we never had any conversations. I didn't report to him."

Jennifer helped herself to a glass of water while Special Agent Ludlow excused himself and left the room. In a minute he returned, smiled at Jennifer, and took his seat. He looked at Jennifer for several seconds before speaking.

"You went to see Mrs. Owens. Was that your own idea or did someone suggest it to you?"

"My own idea."

"I'm still not clear *why* you looked her up. Would you elaborate?"

Jennifer grimaced. "I saw Mr. Owens get killed. I was and still am shocked and revolted by what happened to that man. I felt the need to investigate and see if there was anything I could do for his family and help catch his killer. He was a nice soft-spoken man. Hard to believe..."

Special Agent Ludlow twirled his pen between two fingers and then looked at Jennifer. "In my experience a witness to a violent event usually doesn't seek attention and doesn't try to solve the crime. They give the police all they know, so *they* can do their job to solve the crime."

Jennifer shrugged and examined her fingernails.

"Your ex husband works at Century Design. Has he asked you to investigate this event?"

"He's a partner at Century Design; and no, I have not talked with him about *anything* in ages."

"And, you never had any conversation with Mr. Owens?"

"As I told you before, no."

"Mrs. Owens...did she give you anything when you were there? Papers? Books? Anything?"

Jennifer shook her head. "Just tea." She sighed. "I told you everything. I wasn't there long."

"Long enough to have tea."

"I left right afterward."

"Did Mrs. Owens talk about her husband's work? His job? What he did at Century Design?"

"Only that he was some sort of an accountant. She didn't elaborate."

"How did Mrs. Owens get along with Mr. Downy? When she worked there, I mean."

"Okay, I guess. She hardly mentioned him. I don't know."

"Did you get the opinion she disliked him?" asked Ludlow.

Jennifer shook her head slowly. "No. I don't recall anything like that."

"She didn't ask you what you were doing there, being Mr. Downy's ex wife and all?"

"She said something about that, but I don't recall it exactly. I told her I was interested in finding out who killed her husband, as I saw the whole thing, and that it bothered me." She glared at Ludlow. "*She* didn't act like it was something weird."

Ludlow smiled, nodded and looked at his notebook briefly. "Thank you for coming in. I think you helped clarify some things." He passed a business card across the table. "If you come across anything that could help us in this case, I'd appreciate a call."

Jennifer nodded and took the card. "Are we done?"

Ludlow stood. "Agent Barrow will see you out. Thanks again."

—

The message light was blinking on his phone when Special Agent Ludlow returned to his desk. An agent in the field had left him a message reporting on his assignment. Pursuant to a warrant, a listening device had been installed in Jennifer Wilson's apartment. The active bug had been installed in the base of the lamp on her end table next to the sofa. He went on to explain it could be monitored from the parking lot of the apartment. It was battery operated and recharged from a magnetically coupled circuit to the lamp's power line. Thus, the device would be operating continuously until eventually discovered. He closed by saying; they had not yet had the opportunity to install a device in the Owens's home.

—

Tim started the car as soon as Jennifer closed her door.

"How did it go?" asked Tim.

Jennifer scowled. "I don't know what they were really after. They were all over the place with their questions, and then they re-asked the same ones."

"Were they accusing you of something?"

She shook her head. "It was Special Agent Ludlow doing the talking. A couple other guys in there, but they didn't say anything."

"What do you think they were after?"

"You know, I'm not sure. First I thought they wanted me to fess up to receiving something from Mrs. Owens. But later, I started to think they might be suspicious of Mrs. Owens herself."

"Mrs. Owens? Really? In what way?"

"That's just it. He kept hopping around. I'm not sure what he was thinking. Was she hiding something from them? Or was she involved somehow in her husband's death? It was rather confusing, for me at least."

"Maybe that was their intent. Not tell you what they were after, but try and get what they could from you," said Tim.

Jennifer looked at Tim and smiled. "You're pretty smart. Now, how about buying a girl a drink?"

———

Roy Wilson, Jennifer's uncle, the real estate developer with business interests in Florida and Las Vegas, reported into the Cipriano mob at a high level although he was not a 'made guy.' He lived in a luxurious condo in Burlington and managed his business interests from his home.

Roy had just returned from lunch and picked up his messages when the phone buzzed on his desk. "Hello. Roy Wilson."

"Mister Wilson, this is Frank Cipriano."

Roy gulped. Hearing from Frank directly was highly unusual. "Yes sir. How can I help you?"

"I'd like to talk with you in private. Would you be able to meet me for a drink in Woburn in an hour or so?"

"Sure. Where?"

"You were down here once before meeting with Angelo. Without mentioning it, I'd like to meet you there in an hour. Are you good with that?"

"Yes sir. I'll be there."

"See you then." Frank Cipriano hung up.

Roy walked into the Sand Trap meeting room at the Montvale Country Club and joined Frank Cipriano and several men at a table.

Frank stood up. "Hello Roy. Here, sit down. These gentlemen were just leaving."

The three other men nodded, pushed their chairs back, and got up from the table.

"I'll see you gentlemen in a little while," said Frank. "Have a drink and I'll come find you."

The men acknowledged with a nod and left the room.

Frank smiled at Roy. "Good to see you. You been well?"

"I'm fine," replied Roy. "I want to thank you for a...for your help with... my niece."

Frank nodded. "I couldn't let a threat like that stand. It wasn't something any of my people would do. Dino went out on his own on that and had to pay for it."

"Thanks."

Frank waved it off. Instead, he brought up what he heard about Century Design and the two CDs retrieved from the briefcase carried by Edward Owens.

"Roy, the CDs I saw are labeled as numbers 3 and 4 and have organizational and funds routing information on them. Also, depositors and account managers are identified by name. Needless to say, this information needs to be kept away from the FBI, SEC and IRS investigators."

"Are there copies?"

"Not that we're aware of. However, we believe there are two more CDs out there somewhere, numbers 1 and 2. They have God-knows-what information on them. I *have* to get them from whoever has them."

"You're sure there are more CDs?" asked Roy.

Frank nodded. "The ones we have are labeled 3 and 4. I have to assume that numbers 1 and 2 are out there somewhere. I'm afraid to even think of what could be on them. The whole organization of funds movement might be spelled out on those damn things."

"Jesus..."

"If that's the case, and the FBI gets their hands on them, many people would be going to prison for conspiracy, amongst other charges. The two CDs *must* be located and retrieved. Any copies of the CDs *must* be eliminated."

While listening to Frank, Roy Wilson knew he would be included in any charges of conspiracy to defraud, as he was the main facilitator of money movement from the racketeering and laundering operations in Las Vegas, through the phony Nevada corporation, to Century Design where the monies lost more of their identification as they entered a variety of accounts held by individuals and commercial organizations, as well as Cipriano people.

Roy shook his head. "Downy has always been a loose canon. He and I never saw eye to eye on most things. The way he works scares the crap out of me."

"I know. Worries me, too. But that is where we're going to have to start digging. That's where the problem started. I don't know what this Owens fellow was up to, but we gotta find those two missing CDs. I need you to look into this as quick as you can. I have to get those CDs before someone else does."

"Who are the likely suspects, any ideas?" asked Roy.

Frank shook his head. "I don't know where Owens was taking the CDs he had on him. However, it was likely he was taking them to the person or place where the numbers 1 and 2 CDs were stored. We might be lucky and the FBI doesn't have them yet."

"You had someone look through the Owens house?"

Frank nodded. "The police scrubbed the house and his safe deposit box with a warrant. They listed all the CDs they took. There were a bunch of them, but none were the ones we're looking for."

"I guess if the police found anything like what you describe, we would have heard about it by now," said Roy.

"Bet your ass we would have," said Frank. "We'd all be talking to our lawyers."

"Owens probably gave those CDs to someone. I don't know who at this moment, but there are some suspects that bear scrutiny."

Frank looked at Roy expectantly.

"I'm thinking of Owens's wife," said Roy, "as well as some as-yet unidentified lawyer, investigator, or news reporter."

Frank scowled. "There is also your niece." On seeing the shock on Roy's face, Frank held up a hand. "She was seen in the mall at the time Owens was hit. I can't ignore that. Neither should you."

Roy shook his head slowly.

"Roy, give this serious consideration, and come up with a plan to find those CDs. Do it quickly and keep me informed."

As he left the meeting, Roy knew he couldn't refuse.

CHAPTER 15

Bruce Engelman had spent all day at the Burlington Public Library and his back ached. *Damn wooden chairs.* Sitting in front of the computer, he had perused every financial newssheet in eastern Massachusetts of the past six months. An OPED article in an old financial newspaper had stated Robert Downy inserted himself into a commercial condo project in Salem named Ocean Tower by blackmail. The amount of investment actually made by Downy in the condo project had not been disclosed; leaving Bruce to think the story was probably true. The same OPED stated Downy had gotten photographic proof of an underwriter at a secret apartment in Danvers where he would tryst with his mistress, a local politician's wife. Downy apparently had used the information as leverage into the Ocean Tower project.

Bruce had been told by a freelance operative, who had been sniffing around bars and lounges in the Burlington area, that Downy had had conversations with Angelo Costello, a made guy, regarding possible Cipriano investment in the Ocean Tower condo project. Bruce's interest was piqued. He used pencil and paper to make a diagram of what the Downy organization might look like and to make sense of what the money trails might be. Now, tired, exasperated and hungry, he closed his notebook and left the library.

—

Jennifer sat with Tim in a booth at the *Clover Leaf* lounge in Burlington. When she heard her cell phone buzzing, she retrieved it from her purse. The display showed a phone number she did not immediately recognize.

"Hello."

"Jennifer, this is Roy Wilson."

"Uncle Roy, is something wrong?"

"How have you been? Anybody bothering you?"

"I... I'm okay. Tim's been with me."

"Good. You're still staying at your parent's place?"

"Yes."

"I know we talked about this, but I have to ask again. Please be certain about your answer. It's important to me."

"What is it?" asked Jennifer. She glanced at Tim and shrugged.

"You were in the mall and witnessed Mr. Owens get shot."

"Yes, I told you."

"Just bear with me," said Roy. "You visited Mrs. Owens in her home and she let you look through some of her husband's things."

"Yes, but the police had taken everything."

"Jennifer, I'm told there are two CDs missing in the material recovered from Mr. Owens and from his house. I don't know anymore than that or what it means, but I want to make sure you do not have any knowledge of them. Is this true?"

Jennifer frowned and glanced at Tim.

"What?" whispered Tim.

"I don't have anything belonging to Mr. Owens," said Jennifer. "I told you this already."

"You haven't heard anything about any CDs from anyone?"

"No. What is going on?"

"It's important that these CDs are found. I'm afraid some people will be getting a bit paranoid about them and making trouble for all of us. So, if you come by any knowledge of them, please call me. No questions asked."

"Okay. I will."

"I'll be in touch." Roy hung up.

Jennifer stared at Tim. Her lip trembled.

"What? What did he say?"

"He...he said there'll be trouble...if the CDs aren't found."

"How does he know there *are* any CDs?" asked Tim.

She stared at him. "I... I don't know. How *would* he know?"

"If the cops had found anything incriminating, wouldn't we have heard about it? Wouldn't it have appeared on the list of CDs they seized at the house?"

"Is my uncle involved in this?"

Tim shook his head. "What does he want *you* to do?"

"Maybe he thinks I have them?

"Think about it," stressed Tim. "If Mrs. Owens knew the CDs were there, she sure wouldn't have let you find them and take them."

"Tim, what are you saying?"

"She's the only one who could have known about them other than her husband. And since she obviously doesn't, means there's no trail from *her* to you. The video footage from the mall cameras shows that you did *not* get anything from Owens. Your uncle is probably getting some heat, maybe from Cipriano, to find the CDs. They feel certain there are two somewhere numbered 1 and 2. When the cops opened up his deposit box and searched his belongings, those two CDs weren't there."

"So... you think I'll be safe now?" asked Jennifer.

Tim frowned. "I wish I could say yes, but I don't think so."

"But why?"

"Whoever wants those CDs, and this may go a lot higher than your uncle, will do whatever they have to, to get them. They probably figure that it's highly likely that you, Bruce, or I know about them. Mrs. Owens is a suspect also, I think. I would assume at this point that both your apartment and mine have been bugged, or soon will be. We need to get a guy to search for listening devices."

"In my parents' place?"

"Yep."

"Who can you get to do this?"

"I'll talk to Bruce. He knows a lot of people."

—

Jennifer and Tim opened the door to greet Bruce and a companion. "Hey Bruce, come in." She had told him the code for the gate access when he had called a few minutes earlier.

Bruce stepped inside followed by his friend. "Jennifer, this is Greg Halstead. Greg this is Jennifer and her friend Tim." They all shook hands. "Greg is the guy I mentioned the other day. He's here to check for listening devices. He brought some equipment."

Greg grinned and held up a large plastic toolbox. "It's all in here."

"Greg owns *CamLock* down in Cambridge," said Bruce. "He's good with all the spook devices."

Tim smiled. "Great. It'll be a relief to be sure we're clean."

Jennifer nodded. "Yeah. You guys go ahead and do your thing. Tim and I will watch TV for a while."

Greg, with Bruce tagging along, started in the living room examining all the furniture, the lamps, the TV, and looked behind the covers on the light switches and electric outlets. Greg used a hand-held device to sense for radio frequency devices. On finishing in the living room, they proceeded to the dining and kitchen area and finished in the bedrooms. It took almost an hour to thoroughly check each room.

Greg and Bruce came into the living room grinning.

"The place is clean," declared Greg. "I couldn't detect anything."

"Is that a guarantee?" asked Tom.

"No," said Greg. "But, I'm better than 90 percent sure."

"It doesn't look like anyone's got in here...yet," said Bruce. "Greg said he'd do your own places for free if you give him a few days notice."

"Yeah, sure," said Greg. "I get out this way a lot."

"Mostly private places?" asked Jennifer.

"Most of the screening I do is for individuals. At commercial concerns, I do some installations to keep them secure."

"We appreciate your checking the place out," said Tim.

"Really," echoed Jennifer. "Thanks."

"You're welcome. Can I exit the gate without a problem?"

Jennifer smiled. "It'll open for you. A key code is only needed to come in."

Greg went to the door, waved, and left.

The three friends sat at the dining room table in discussion and trying to understand the apparently interconnected entities and flow of money associated with Century Design. Bruce showed the Power Point charts he had started to develop on his laptop screen.

"I just want the killer of Mr. Owens brought to justice," said Jennifer. "He was assassinated, and I have to ask why."

"Maybe to shut him up," suggested Bruce. "But there was a witness. You. Whoever *ordered* the hit on Owens found out about you, and they don't want any loose ends to come back and bite them."

Jennifer shook her head. "I thought I was in danger from Owens's killer, but now I'm in danger from who? Having those two CDs could be bad for my health."

Tim looked at Jennifer. "Should we destroy them and not pursue this any further?"

Jennifer looked back and forth from Tim to Bruce. "What should I do?"

"As long as some bad guy *thinks* you have them, or thinks you have seen what's on them, then you'll be in danger," said Tim.

"I think he's right," said Bruce. "If you destroy them, they'll still be looking for them and wondering who may have seen what's on them. If you give them to these creeps, they'll wonder if you have seen what's on them and whether you have copies of them."

"Give them to my uncle?" asked Jennifer.

Bruce shook his head. "The guy that eventually ends up with them will be wondering..."

"How about sending them to the FBI?" asked Tim.

"Will they accuse you of hiding them? And where did you get them?" said Bruce. "It'd be a can of worms. Maybe if you sent them anonymously..."

Tim saw Jennifer's lip tremble. She looked at him. "What should I do?"

"I think we should figure out how these organizations work and how they're tied together. I'm sure there's a tie-in to the Cipriano people. Maybe if we figure how this works, we can make a better decision about the CDs. Maybe we do give them to the FBI. But, let's understand what it all means first, so none of us gets in any more trouble."

"What trouble?" said Jennifer.

"We did lie to the FBI. It's a felony."

Jennifer nodded and looked at Bruce. "What do you think?"

"From studying the CDs, I think someone is going to be desperate about getting their hands on them. They tell a very convoluted story of what I think is money laundering and fraud."

Jennifer shook her head. "If only I left them there, then Downy or Roy Wilson would have found them. Maybe Mrs. Owens would have found them. In any case, no one would be looking at me."

Tim put his hand on hers. "Your right. However, *you* have them now, and we need to think what the right thing to do is."

He turned to look at Bruce. "Let's go over the details you have so we all understand the system."

Bruce nodded and leaned back in the sofa. "I've been studying the reports in the financial sheets at the library, digging through the Internet as well as newspapers going back a few years. To make a long story short, it seems that Century Design was started by Bob Downy to be simply a Ponzi scheme."

"I don't even want to hazard a guess as to why his early big investors died. However, ever since then Downy has been advertising a return to his investors of at least two points above the best dividend rates in the market. That's why he has so many investors, both big and small. But if you do the math, and I'm pretty good at it, he can't keep paying that rate of return when he only earns market rates of interest. It's got to be a Ponzi scheme... or something else."

"How the heck does he keep it up?" asked Tim looking at Bruce.

"Unlike some more famous Ponzi schemes, Downy doesn't give outrageous payouts. As long as he keeps getting new money, he can keep making the payouts and skimming to feather his own nest."

Tim nodded. "Until new money slows down."

Bruce continued, "I've been thinking. Since Cipriano started running things, and likely using Century to conceal, confuse and launder the earnings of his outfit, then it would seem to me it would be in his interest to keep a lot of new money coming in from other investors; thus, the good interest rate. Also, should Century need some cash in a market slowdown to make payout to investors, Cipriano could pony up some of their own cash, and just consider it as a cost-of-doing-business in order to keep his laundry operation running."

Tim grinned. "You're smarter than you look."

"It's about time you noticed."

"Century and Cipriano must've been operating like this for some time," said Tim.

Bruce nodded. "They have. Back in the financial mess of 2008, Downy wasn't able to bring in enough new investors, while quite a few withdrew their funds out of fear or necessity. In any event, that's when Cipriano came into the picture."

"You mean he had an account there...with Downy?" asked Jennifer.

"I haven't wrapped my head around all this; but it appears that there are several Cipriano accounts at Century linked to a company in Nevada. Turns out this company is a shell company with the ownership not made public."

"They can do that?" asked Tim.

Bruce nodded. "It turns out the USA is the only country where it is possible to incorporate a shell corporation, in Delaware and Nevada, without the identity of the owner being registered."

"That's just legalized fraud. Isn't it?" said Tim.

Bruce shrugged. "I guess the politicians wanted somewhere to stash *their* money."

"Unbelievable," Jennifer commented.

Tim looked at Bruce. "So, what are you saying about Century Design... and Downy?"

Bruce glanced at Tim and Jennifer and then at his computer. "Here's what it looks like to me. First of all, money from Cipriano's Las Vegas operations gets funneled into a company called Nevada Enterprises."

Tim interrupted. "What do *they* do?"

"Nevada Enterprises breaks up the large amounts of cash into less conspicuous smaller sums, just under ten-grand, that are then deposited directly into various accounts in a lot of different US banks. The monies from *these* accounts are then deposited into accounts at Century Design." Bruce looked at Tim. "Interestingly, it appears from what I can surmise, the monies coming into Century from these various banks are deposited into just a few *common* accounts together with private and institutional moneys."

Jennifer shook her head. "I'm getting a head ache."

"Yeah, so am I," said Tim.

"It's simple," said Bruce. "I don't know how legal it is, but when you dump all the moneys from all parties into just a few investment accounts, the identity of the ownership is lost. This way, the ownership of the moneys in the funds is according to however they set it up on their books. I guess, as long as everyone keeps getting above market returns, no one complains. If someone wants to cash out, then Century has to pay them their investment value, whatever they came in with."

"Where does Century invest their moneys?" asked Tim.

"So far, I've identified eight global banks where funds are deposited to earn interest. This further obfuscates the sources of the funds."

"There must be others investing in Century Design," said Tim.

"Oh, there is," said Bruce. "Wilson Property Development has accounts at Century. Ocean Tower, managed by Wilson, has an account at Century. And, there is a whole list of private and institutional investors."

Jennifer shook her head. "You're saying Bob Downy owns Century Design and is in charge of all this? Unbelievable."

Bruce shook his head. "Not exactly. When he started to go under in 2008, Cipriano came in with a bucket of cash and installed a new partner, guy named Mario Russo. He's the guy keeping an eye on Downy and making sure Cipriano money is safe. From that day on, Downy really works for Cipriano."

"Wow. This is amazing," said Jennifer. "But it still begs the question."

Bruce and Tim stared at her.

"Who ordered Mr. Owens to be killed?" Jennifer looked at them. "I want to know."

"Probably the same people that want the two CDs," replied Tim.

"But who is that?" asked Jennifer. "Is it Downy? Is it Cipriano? I don't think its Roy Wilson."

"Downy would be more likely to know about Owens and the CDs than anybody else. Hell, Owens worked for him," said Bruce. "Downy might have discovered something suspicious that Owens was doing that would incriminate him. So, he asked one of the Cipriano guys to have Owens followed and they whacked him on the way to the bank and grabbed the briefcase."

Jennifer sighed. "It's beginning to make *some* sense, but I don't know..."

"I wonder if Owens intended for the four CDs to go to the FBI?" said Tim.

"Maybe," said Bruce. "Or to blackmail Downy?"

"That suggests Downy was doing something iffy," said Jennifer.

"You think he might be skimming from Century? Why? How?" said Tim. "If he got caught at it wouldn't Cipriano be the one coming after him?"

"There's more questions than answers," said Bruce. "I still don't know about the earlier deaths associated with Century. I haven't been able to learn much at the library or Internet."

"What *do you* know about it?" asked Tim.

Bruce sighed. "About five years ago this guy, Richard Engels, made a sizable investment in Century. I'm not sure, but it had to have been several million. Anyway, one day he was out on his cabin cruiser off of Cape Cod when the boat blew up. It burned to the water line. No one ever saw Engels again and he was declared dead."

"I heard about it," said Jennifer.

"So, Century ended up with the millions?" asked Tim.

"It seems so, from what I could find," said Bruce. "They had some sort of business arrangement where the monies stayed with the company if anything were to happen to either one of them. I haven't figured that out yet."

"How convenient," said Jennifer.

Bruce raised his eyebrows. "Then a few years ago, Ron Feldman came along. He had a bucket of money and they made him a partner in Century. It wasn't long before he died of heart failure. The police suspected poisoning, but the cops botched the evidence and they haven't been able to prove it. The DA still has the case listed as open."

"Holy cow. And I was married to that guy?" Jennifer shook her head.

"I wonder if Cipriano was involved in any of this?" asked Tim.

Bruce shrugged. "You can bet the FBI knows."

CHAPTER 16

Elaine Owens, standing by the window with a drink in her hand, saw the gray car stop in front of her house. Two men in dark suits got out, one of them with a briefcase, and started up the walkway to her door. She gulped the rest of her cocktail, put the glass on a coaster, and straightened her blouse. There was a knock on the door.

She opened the door to the limit of the safety chain. "Yes?"

"Mrs. Owens, I am FBI Special Agent Brian Ludlow and this is Agent Grant Foster. We'd appreciate fifteen minutes of your time to help clarify some details concerning your deceased husband."

Elaine looked from one to the other and then at the ID they held up. She nodded and undid the safety chain from the door. "Come in."

The two men entered her living room and introduced each other again and shook hands. Elaine gestured toward the sofa. "Please. Sit down."

The agents sat and Ludlow removed a notebook from his briefcase. He retrieved a voice recorder and placed it on the coffee table in front of him, then looked up at Elaine. "We'd like to record our conversation, make sure we get it right."

Elaine nodded and sat in the chair close to the window. She glanced at her empty cocktail glass, and then folded her hands in her lap. "Do I need a lawyer?"

"I don't know why," said Ludlow. "You're not under arrest. You may terminate this meeting at any time. We would appreciate your help, however."

"Okay." She looked at Ludlow. "What can I do for you?"

"It seems to us, the motivation for the attack on your husband was to obtain the briefcase he was carrying."

"But...but they *killed* him," she exclaimed.

Ludlow nodded. "Yes. I'm sorry. But we think it was to obtain the briefcase. Frankly, we're not real clear why Mr. Owens was killed. We don't think it was the primary intent."

Elaine shook her head. "It doesn't make sense. Who would do that?"

"Did your husband have enemies at Century Design?"

She shook her head. "No."

"Did your husband uncover some malfeasance or irregularity, maybe involving Mr. Downy?"

"What? No. He never told me..."

"Where did you meet your husband?"

Elaine pursed her lips. "It must've been four years ago, now. I was doing some accounting at Century Design. Edward was the head accountant. I reported to him."

"You haven't worked there in the last four months. Mind telling us why you left?" asked Ludlow.

Elaine shrugged. "Bored, I guess. We didn't need the money. Edward had a good salary."

"Did you leave on good terms with Mr. Downy?"

She nodded. "He and Edward and I were friends, went out once in a while."

"Do you still see him; he still a friend?"

"He's been over once since Edward passed away. We talked for a while."

Ludlow looked at Elaine. "Please forgive me. I have to ask some personal questions...so we can get a good overall picture."

Elaine glanced at her empty glass, scowled and nodded.

"Would you say your marriage was good, average, or not so good?"

Grant Foster repositioned himself on the sofa and looked away from Elaine.

"Well," said Elaine, "I would say it was average. Yes, average."

"And you both have been in good health?"

"Usual aches and pains."

"Were there any financial difficulties?"

Elaine gave Ludlow a hard look. "What the heck you need all this for. This is kind of over the top."

Ludlow straightened his posture. "I'm sorry Mrs. Owens. We appreciate getting all this information now. Saves *you* having to come down to headquarters. A thorough investigation of your husband's death, and determining who was involved and why, requires us to do a detailed survey of everyone in your husband's recent life. All of this stays in the file. It is not public information."

She shook her head. "What else is on your mind?"

"Records show you have one joint bank account; two credit card accounts and Mr. Owens had an IRA account. Is this accurate?"

She nodded. "Yes."

"Are there life insurance policies?"

"We each had 25,000 dollars."

"You and your husband have any other property?"

Elaine shook her head. "We sold the bungalow on the Cape about eight months ago. We didn't use it very much."

"Do you own your home here?"

"Yes. It is paid off, and the car is paid off as well."

"Have you or Mr. Owens spent much time at the casinos in Connecticut or New Jersey?"

She scowled. "That was never our thing."

Ludlow looked directly at Elaine. "Please don't be offended by my next questions. I'm required to ask."

Elaine shook her head and scowled. "Let's get this meeting over with."

"Did Mr. Owens have a lover?"

"There was never any hint of it."

"And you, Mrs. Owens? Have you had or do you have a lover."

"Oh, for Christ sakes! No. I haven't. Are we done yet?"

"Forgive me. A few more and we'll be done."

Elaine sighed. "Let's finish."

"Are there any children or aged parents depending on your help?"

"No. Edward's parents are gone. Mine are in a retirement place in Florida."

"Do you have *any* idea what your husband was doing at the mall that day?"

Elaine shook her head. "I just don't know. Our account was not with that bank."

"And neither of you were planning any traveling in the near term?"

Elaine scowled. "No."

"As you've already been told, the police found his passport, $46,000 cash, and a one-way ticket to Miami. What do you make of that?"

Elaine shook her head slowly. Her lip trembled. "I wish I knew."

"No idea at all?" pressed Ludlow.

"No. Are we done now?"

Ludlow closed his notebook and Foster turned off the recorder and slipped it into his jacket pocket.

"Mrs. Owens, this has been a great help. I apologize for the questions." Ludlow and Foster walked to the door.

Elaine stood, but didn't offer to open the door.

Foster pulled the door open, smiled and walked out. Ludlow thanked her again and left.

At the window, Elaine watched them through the open blinds. When the car departed, she picked up the cocktail glass and went into the kitchen. Her hands were trembling as she prepared another drink.

—

Ludlow started the car and glanced at Foster. "First thing she asked was whether she needed a lawyer. That was kind of odd."

"Yeah, especially since we hadn't asked her anything."

Ludlow scratched his chin. "I can almost believe her, except when it comes to Mr. Downy."

"Really? I didn't catch anything."

"No, you wouldn't have. You were looking at her boobs instead of her face."

Foster scowled. "Give me a break."

"When I asked about Downy, she lost the stony look she had throughout our conversation."

"You think she and Downy...?"

"That's what I would like to find out," said Ludlow. "This situation may have several other dimensions."

"Yeah. Why the hell kill the guy if all you wanted was the briefcase?" said Foster.

"We need to figure out what her relationship with her husband was *really* like. Don't you think?" asked Ludlow.

Foster nodded. "There are lots of loose ends."

CHAPTER 17

Bruce drove toward Salem, MA while questions fought for his attention. What're the long-range plans for these dip-shits, he wondered. Why kill old man Owens? And then whack his killer? What was that really about? Is this all about some CDs? For Cipriano, it's gotta be about money coming into the outfit. For Downy, is it about some illegal activity? Or, is he squirreling money in some offshore bank? If so, for what? Is he gonna flee to another country? Does he have a mistress? And, what the hell does Roy Wilson have to do in all this?

In Salem, Bruce turned into the parking lot in front of the Ocean Tower building. The lot seemed oddly empty for a twelve-story building, but then he saw an underground parking garage with key code access. He counted only a dozen cars parked at the front of the building. He parked and then walked toward the building with notebook and smart-phone in hand.

When he tugged on the glass doors, they didn't budge. There was a key code/card scanner on each side of the doors, as well as a directory under glass. Bruce took a photo of the listings. The twelve-story building showed only eleven tenants. No one was shown to be on the top two floors. On the main floor there was a listing for Building Manager, Building Engineer, and Business Office. There were no names following these titles. The same phone number was shown for all three offices.

A well-dressed man walked up to the doors, nodded at Bruce, and scanned his key card. Bruce heard the door unlock. The man entered and pulled the door shut behind him without looking at Bruce. The man disappeared into the elevator. Bruce watched the dial spin up and stop on the 9th floor. He looked at the register to read, Turner Enterprises. He'd have to look that up when he got home, he decided.

Sitting in his car, Bruce entered each name from the photo of the register at the Ocean Tower lobby into the Internet search engine of his smartphone. Every entry returned a one-page exposition showing a photo of the Ocean Tower building with the name of the presumed tenant and a telephone number highlighted in a text box. Bruce called several of the numbers and received a recording in each case directing the caller to leave a message. He wondered whether there were any real tenants in these suites.

Tim and Jennifer had invited Bruce to join them at the Pizza Hut in Chelmsford. Bruce took the opportunity to bring his friends up to date on what he had been doing during the last couple days. "I don't know about you guys, but I've been busy."

Tim grinned. "What's her name?"

Jennifer glanced up from her pizza slice. "You have a girlfriend?"

"When do I have time?" Bruce shook his head. "I've been checking out the Ocean Tower building out in Salem, along with other stories that actually pay me money."

Tim and Jennifer looked at him. "Really? Ocean Tower? How come?" asked Jennifer.

Bruce swallowed a third of a slice of pizza, and then chased it with a long sip of diet soda. "From what I've already read, it seems to me Downy or Cipriano might be laundering money through Ocean Tower."

Tim looked puzzled. "They just built that. How do you know?"

"I was over there yesterday and checked it out. I took a picture of the Directory. Then, I searched each name on Goggle as well as Yahoo on my phone. Every entry returned a page showing a photo of the Ocean Tower building with the name of the presumed tenant and a telephone number. I called each of these numbers. In every case I got a canned recording telling me to leave a message. I don't think most of these business suites are occupied."

Tim looked up from his plate. "Doesn't mean they're laundering money there. Why do you think that?"

Bruce shrugged. "No real proof; not yet anyway. But what a good setup to do just that. Think about it. A new building. Fill it up with new furniture and start renting the suites out to clients." Bruce raised his eyebrows. "Except here's the catch: suppose the lessees are fake. They keep the suites empty for a period of time, maybe years. Nothing gets damaged or worn out, but you are constantly invoicing customers. Money comes into Ocean Tower, all be it from nefarious sources. Ocean Tower looks very profitable. If you want to sell the place at some point, you can get a good price based on the profitability of the lessees, on paper at least. I'm not saying that is what's happening, but it seems like it could be."

Jennifer looked at Bruce. "You think my dip-shit ex is doing this?"

Bruce nodded. "If he is, he's likely doing it under the direct control of Cipriano. It'd be his money being laundered."

"Wow. You really outdid yourself this time," exclaimed Tim.

"Yeah, and you're not even paying me."

"You're the man," Tim rejoined.

"Of course he is," smiled Jennifer.

CHAPTER 18

Mario Russo was looking after the Cipriano interests at Century Design. This morning Frank had asked him to come to his office. Mario knocked on the open office door. When Frank gestured, he walked in and took a seat in front of his desk.

Frank smiled and reached to shake Mario's hand. "Mario, how are things going over there?"

Mario grinned and shook his head. "Downy wants me to think everything is just great. I've only been over there a month. However, keeping an eye on the flow of funds and trying to reconcile the myriad of paperwork, has just about convinced me Downy is skimming a large amount of money from the company."

Frank's face turned dark. "Whacha got?"

"I'm fully aware the purposefully obfuscated management of all monies coming into Century Design is to hide the true sources and destinations of our invested funds. However, these methods make skimming of funds relatively easy since tracking money movement *within* the company is designed to be impossible."

"Downy is a sleaze. Eventually he will have to go. What have you learned?"

"I think well over 300-grand has been skimmed in this calendar year alone."

"You sure?" asked Frank.

"Ninety percent. Like I said, it is *designed* to be impossible for anyone to figure it out."

Frank nodded. "This might be a valuable lesson for us if we can figure out what he's doing. We gotta make sure *no one* can figure out what's happening internally, especially the feds."

"I'm trying to find things out without making Downy suspicious," said Mario.

Frank nodded. "Can you, by yourself and no one else, design a tracking system that tells you when monies are being moved? It's got to be a tracking system that can be removed at a moment's notice if state or federal inspectors show up. It can't leave any footprints."

"I've been thinking some about it. I could build a program or set of programs on my own private laptop. Then at the office, I could plug my laptop into the desktop unit. That way all the spook program stuff stays on my private unit and when I disconnect from the office unit, no one is the wiser. I don't leave any useful footprints."

"You're smarter than you look. How soon can it be done?"

"Do you think your son could help me? He's studying to be a software engineer. Right?"

Frank nodded.

"If we had a small office here, he and I could develop the necessary programs without prying eyes. If Downy showed up here, I'd just say we're doing stuff for his college work."

"I'll talk to him in the next couple days. Meantime, get started with your idea," said Frank.

"I wouldn't trust Downy as far as I could throw him," said Mario. "You really need him around?"

"Downy, as a front man for Century Design, serves my needs right now. Investors know him. However, this shit, if it's true, won't go unpunished. You gather up all the evidence of his skimming and when the time is right, I'll hang it around his neck, maybe as a gift to federal inspectors."

Mario nodded and grinned. "By the way, I've seen several incoming messages for Downy on the secretary's desk from a guy named Ed DiCosta. That name mean anything top you?"

Frank shook his head slowly. "The DiCosta outfit in Rhode Island has been trying to get Century Design to open an account for them for over a year. They say they have upwards of ten million to invest."

Mario frowned. "What did you tell them?"

"I told Downy in no uncertain terms that he was *not* to open an account or accept money from the DiCosta outfit. With that kind of investment, DiCosta would soon demand a position in governing the company, and then they'd attempt a complete takeover. They have a lot of muscle and resources."

"That'd give them a toehold in the Boston area."

"Yeah. They've been wanting that for a long time," said Frank. "I would like you to report to me immediately about any further activity by DiCosta. Don't wait. I want to know right away." Frank picked up his phone.

"Will do." Mario left the office.

FBI Agent Foster entered Special Agent Ludlow's office and sat down in front of his desk uninvited.

Ludlow looked up. "Make yourself at home." Then he scowled.

"I think I just did."

"Have you been looking into Downy and Owens?" asked Ludlow.

Foster nodded. "I was eyeballing the Owens place yesterday and saw Downy arrive in his own car. In a few minutes they both came out of the house and took off. They ended up at Eduardo's Restaurant on the other side of the mall in Burlington."

"Yeah, I know where it is."

"I went in and sat at the bar. I watched them for a while and left before they did. They were sure cozy, had a booth in the back and sat next to each other."

Ludlow smiled. "Consoling the widow?"

"Definitely. No doubt there is a relationship there. It may have started a while back. Her late husband might have found out."

"And what; you think that was the reason for murder?"

Foster shook his head. "No. The mall thing was a very risky, even foolish, operation. No, it wasn't because she was cheating on him. I'm sure the purpose was the briefcase. Killing him was a sloppy deal. I'm not sure why he was killed."

"Yeah. Looked like an amateur thing...but, maybe not."

"There's a lot of small-time shooters out there that'd do a job like that for small change," said Foster. "May not be part of the mob scene."

Ludlow raised an eyebrow. "Or, maybe it is."

"Why do you say that?"

"We know there is a connection between Downy and Cipriano. We're just not real sure how it's hooked up."

"So, what would be the motive? Something in that briefcase he carried?"

Ludlow scowled. "Grab the briefcase, sure. But why was he killed? And why was the shooter killed...and by who?"

"I was able to get the judge to okay the paperwork for the landline phone at the Owen's house. I also have a request for Downy and Owens's cell phone records. It'll probably be a couple more days."

"Anything show up on the Owens's home phone?"

"I've got calls to and from Mrs. Owens and Downy every couple of days. They last about twenty minutes and occur between 8 and 5pm on weekdays. These calls have been going on for the past year. Gotta wonder if her husband knew about it, maybe saw the phone records."

"I'm wondering if he even cared," said Ludlow. "Maybe he had his own thing going."

"Owens had a new passport. His wife had one dated the same as Downy's, about a year ago."

"Interesting."

"I looked at the police report of Owens's home computer. There's evidence of visits to travel web sites, particularly to Central America and the Caribbean region, dating back over a year. Don't know if it was he or she. Our people took a look at Owens's office computer, but it didn't show any travel sites. Kinda begs the question, why a ticket to Miami?"

"Does Downy have any other girl friends?" asked Ludlow.

Foster smiled and stood. "I'll be in touch."

—

The three friends were still at the Pizza Hut in Chelmsford when Bruce placed paper copies of the charts he had made on the table. They illustrated how he saw the organization of Century Design.

Jennifer looked at Bruce. "You got all this from looking at the CDs?"

"That's where I started. I dug through references in the library, web sites, and the Thomas Register."

"What's the Thomas Register?" asked Tim.

"The library had a hard-copy set and it's also available on-line. The database covers both public and private companies. It includes company name, address, telephone number, and fax number, all kinds of stuff. It covers practically every product and service available in the U.S. and Canada."

"Is Century Design listed there?" asked Jennifer.

"Yep. It's a pretty skimpy entry. It does say that Downy is President/CEO and it is a privately held investment company having eighteen full time employees. It doesn't mention any other officers, however."

"Does it say who the principal investors are?" asked Tim.

Bruce shook his head. "And, there are no publicly reported earnings. I guess they don't have to, being private and all."

Tim looked at the charts and then at Bruce. "What do we know about Nevada Enterprises and Ocean Tower? They're separate companies, aren't they?"

"Interestingly, Nevada Enterprises is in a similar business to Century. It is privately held, but since it is registered in Nevada, it doesn't have to publicly state who owns it."

"So, your thinking the Cipriano people really control what happens at Nevada Enterprises as well as at Century?" asked Tim.

"And at Ocean Tower, also. From what I can find out, Century bought a controlling interest in Ocean Tower, and then Cipriano bought the rest of it."

"So, what exactly is Ocean Tower?" asked Jennifer.

"On paper it is an investment company, very much like Century, but for commercial property," said Bruce. "Physically, it seems to me to be a near-empty building. It might lease office space to different businesses. But I just don't know, yet. I need to go back there and poke around a little."

"Maybe you better take me with you," said Tim.

"Okay. I could use another pair of eyes."

"What about my uncle's business, Wilson Property Development?" asked Jennifer.

Bruce looked in his notebook. "The Register lists it as a privately held company with Roy Wilson as President. They employ 34 people between his home office here, Las Vegas and in Florida."

"How does that company fit in with Century?" asked Jennifer. "It does, doesn't it?"

"The only clue is in some of the accounts shown in the CDs you have," said Bruce. "There is an account at Century labeled as Wilson Property."

"So, Century Design is at the center of this enterprise?" asked Tim.

"Yep. Interestingly, there are no accounts at Century labeled Nevada Enterprises, but there are lots of accounts *to* different US banks. I can't prove it yet, but I think the monies from Nevada Enterprises gets to Century by way of a bunch of different banks here in the US."

Jennifer shook her head. "Let's back up for a minute. I really want to know why Mr. Owens got killed. That's what I *really* want to know."

"Maybe for the same reason we have guys coming after us for the CDs," said Tim. "The stuff we are discovering on them could probably send them away for a long time."

"And it all started with Mr. Owens," added Bruce. "I think we've hardly scratched the surface."

"So, Mr. Owens was killed because he stole company secrets and put them on CDs?" asked Jennifer. "Why did he do that? Had to be a reason."

"I can think of a couple," said Tim. "For instance, he might have wanted to blackmail Downy. Or, he could have been working with the feds to get the goods on Downy as well as the Cipriano outfit."

"He had a plane ticket to Miami in his possession and a bunch of money and his passport," said Jennifer. "Sounds more like he was running. But from what or who?"

"That sounds like he was blackmailing Downy and the CDs were his insurance policy," said Bruce. "He might have wanted out of his life – his marriage and Century Design."

"But who engineered the hit?" asked Tim.

"My money is on Downy with help from the Cipriano guys," replied Bruce.

"Wonder if there was a woman involved?" suggested Tim.

Bruce shook his head. "I don't know."

"The cops have his phone records. I bet they know," said Jennifer. "Mrs. Owens claimed there wasn't; but then would she have admitted it to me?"

"I gotta say again; he was very likely blackmailing Downy and the CDs were his insurance policy." Bruce looked at Jennifer and Tim. "We stay here much longer, I'm gonna want another pizza."

Tim grinned. "That does it. We're leaving." He slid out of the booth. "You're gonna call me when you go over to Ocean Tower?"

Bruce nodded. "Yep. Maybe tomorrow."

CHAPTER 19

The day after the friends met at Pizza Hut; Angelo Costello listened attentively to the sounds in his headset while parked nearby the apartment of Jennifer Wilson. He reached to the passenger seat and turned on the voice recorder. This was certainly getting interesting, he thought.

Listening bugs had been installed recently in both the Wilson and Beckman apartments. Frank Cipriano had insisted on knowing where the mystery CDs were, and that he, Angelo, was to retrieve them. Moments before, Angelo had seen Robert Downy drive up to Jennifer's apartment, and had seen him push his way in when the woman opened the door. He had heard a shriek in his headset and then the door closed with a bang.

He now heard Downy's voice clearly. "I don't know how, but you've got them. Give them to me now and I'll leave."

"Get out of here! I'll call the cops."

Angelo heard the panic in her voice.

"Goddamn it. No one else could have them but you. The old man gave them to you, didn't he? Is that why you were in the mall...to get the other CDs?" Downy was yelling now. "Give them to me."

Angelo listened intently, not wanting to miss any clues in the angry banter between Jennifer and Downy. Just then another car pulled up at the apartment. He recognized Tim Beckman as he stepped out of the car.

"Oh shit, now this is trouble," he mumbled. He watched as Beckman went to the apartment entrance and stood there seemingly listening to the loud voices from inside. Then, with his fist, he pounded on the door.

Angelo saw the door open slightly and Beckman push his way in. The door slammed shut. He could still hear the yelling between the woman and Downy, but he couldn't make sense of it. Then he heard Beckman shout, "What the hell is he doing here?"

Jennifer yelled, "He won't leave. Bastard won't go."

"I came here for those CDs, goddamn it. I want them now. Then I'll leave."

Angelo recognized Downy's belligerent voice.

"There are no CDs here. Now piss off and get the hell out," shouted Beckman.

Then Angelo heard a commotion of grunts, thumps, and swearing. Then came a hard thump and what sounded like a crash into furniture. There came more grunts and cursing and a solid thump, followed by two seconds of gasping and more grunting. Angelo saw the door open and Downy stagger out and grab hold of the railing. He turned and yelled into the apartment. "You're going to regret this, asshole...you and your girl friend. Bitch, you had your chance."

The apartment door slammed shut and then Angelo heard, "Goddamn him!" from Jennifer. Angelo watched as Downy staggered to his car with one hand rubbing the back of his neck.

Angelo heard Tom, "Are you okay?"

"I'm so glad you came in just then," said Jennifer. "He was acting crazy."

"He thinks you have the CDs."

Angelo heard what sounded like whispers. He wondered if they were on to the bug or just being careful? Didn't the guy say *the CDs*? Goddamn! They *gotta* know something.

"He sounded desperate," said Jennifer.

"Somebody's leaning on him."

"He's gonna be trouble."

"Yeah, for sure," said Tim. "But he doesn't really know. He's guessing."

"What should we do?"

"Nothing for now. Let me get this guy over here to do a scan for bugs. We gotta be careful what we say."

"Okay. You going to call him?" asked Jennifer.

"Not from here."

Angelo heard noises of movement and then quiet. Did they go into the bedroom, he wondered? *You going to call him? Who the hell is he? Is it that nosy-ass reporter? Shit, a security guy will surely find the damn bug I put in there.*

Angelo opened his phone and pushed the speed dial for Frank Cipriano.

"Hello."

"This is Angelo. Okay to talk?"

"Yeah, but keep it short."

"I was setting up to listen to the woman at her place. Who do you suppose shows up?"

"You gonna tell me or what?"

"It was Downy. He barged into her apartment and demanded *the* CDs. She screamed at him to get out, that she didn't have any CDs. That's when her stud pony came through the door."

"Who?"

"Beckman. He goes in there, and next I hear this yelling and commotion and Downy comes out nursing his neck. I guess he got the worse of it."

"What did you learn? Anything?" asked Frank.

"Her and boyfriend were careful what they said. I recorded it. From what I heard, I'm pretty sure they have the CDs or know where they are. Also, they're gonna get someone to scan for bugs."

"So, you didn't learn shit."

"How aggressive do you want I should get? I'm thinking maybe try a little something on that damn reporter."

"That's already happening. No, you stick with those two. Catch every word."

"Okay, Frank."

—

"Whata dump," said Nick Caruso as he sat down on the sofa. "Shit, we tore the place apart, didn't find squat. Not even a damn Playboy. Hey Tony, what kinda reporter don't have a stack of Playboy's?"

Antonio Cipriano chuckled and shrugged. He picked up magazines and papers from a leather chair and dropped them on the floor, and then eased his bulk into the comfortable cushions. "Can't get into his computer. We'll just hafta wait 'till he comes home."

"He won't be happy to see us."

"I'm supposed to give a shit?" Antonio scowled. "We'll convince him to let us into the computer."

Nick nodded. "Be a good time to see what's in his briefcase and empty out his pockets. We *gotta* find somethin'."

Antonio put a finger to his lips. "Shh. He's at the door."

The door pushed open, and Bruce stood in the doorway, mouth ajar. "What the hell...?" He stared wide-eyed at two men wearing ski masks and latex gloves.

Antonio, now on his feet, pulled a pistol from his back. He grabbed Bruce by the arm and yanked him into the room, kicking the door shut. "We've been expecting you. Made ourselves at home."

"What the hell you guys want?" Bruce looked at the gun. "Who the hell are you?"

Antonio pushed Bruce into the sofa. Nick stood up.

"Bruce baby, you've been making our boss way too nervous and irritable," said Antonio. "You're not gonna want to keep doing that."

Bruce tried to stand, but Nick pushed him back into the sofa.

"Who are you guys? Whatdoya want? What the hell did you do to my place?" Bruce made another attempt to stand, only to be pushed back into the sofa.

Antonio shook his head. "We had us a look around while you were gone. Didn't find what we want, so now you're going to unlock the computer for us."

"Bullshit. Who the hell you think you are? Get out of my apartment." He glanced often at the gun.

Antonio looked at Nick and nodded. Nick took a step toward Bruce and slapped him hard across the face.

Antonio grinned. "You paying attention now?" He put the pistol under his belt at his back.

Bruce rubbed his face and blinked his eyes several times. "You bastards."

"Here's what we're gonna do." Antonio looked at Nick. "You're gonna stand up."

Nick grabbed Bruce by the arm and pulled him to his feet.

"And now you're gonna get that computer up and running," said Antonio. "Any bullshit and it will become very painful."

Bruce was pulled to the computer by Nick and shoved into the chair. "Crank it up. Don't screw with us."

Antonio stood directly behind Bruce and watched his every move. When the Windows program loaded, he said, "Okay, Bruce baby. Get up and go sit on the sofa." He looked at Nick and nodded.

Nick pulled on Bruce's arm and tugged him toward the sofa and pushed him into it. "Get comfy. We'll be looking through your files. Making sure there ain't somethin' there that'll make our boss uncomfortable."

"What the shit you looking for?" asked Bruce. "Who the hell are you?"

Nick glared at Bruce. "It'd be best you just shut up and sit there."

"Assholes." Bruce watched as Antonio pulled a small thumb drive from his pocket and inserted it into a USB port on the front of the computer. "What the hell you doing?"

Nick glared at Bruce. "Told you to shut up."

Bruce folded his arms over his chest and sat quietly for a few minutes.

"Got anything over there?" asked Nick, not mentioning Antonio's name.

"Maybe. I'm copying it all and we'll sift through it later." Antonio turned to Nick. "Check his briefcase."

Nick got up and went to the door where Bruce had dropped his briefcase. He picked it up, held it open, and turned it upside down letting the contents spill on the floor. He checked the interior pockets with his hands before tossing the briefcase across the room.

"You bastards," mumbled Bruce.

Nick dropped to his knees and examined the items but kept Bruce in sight. His fingers closed on a thumb drive and raised it to inspect it. He stood and handed it to Antonio. "Might want to take a look at this."

Antonio took Bruce's thumb drive and inserted it into another USB port of the computer, and then examined the contents list on the screen. It was nearly a minute before he said anything, as he seemed to study several pages intently.

"What's on there?" asked Nick.

"Holy crap," exclaimed Antonio. "I can't believe this. He's trying to describe the whole organization in flow charts...and money trails, too."

"What? The outfit?"

"Yeah." Antonio turned to look at Bruce. "Where did this information come from?"

Bruce scowled but didn't answer.

Nick, now standing, reached to Bruce and slapped him hard across the face. "Hey! Pay attention! He asked you a question."

Bruce rubbed his face, wiping tears from one eye.

"Where did you get this information?" asked Antonio again.

Bruce looked at Antonio. "I'm an investigative reporter. I investigate. It's what I do."

Nick shook his head. "This is gonna get painful for you, Brucie. Better you give us some plain answers."

Antonio scowled. "Let's try it this way. Why are you investigating these businesses?"

"Tryin' to figure out how it all works, how it's interconnected."

"Why? For who? Who's paying you?" asked Antonio.

"It's an investigative piece for the Boston Eagle," lied Bruce.

"The Eagle is paying you for all this? These graphs and detail? Names and places?"

Bruce nodded. "Yep. Get paid when I get it done and send it in."

"They want you to do this?" asked Antonio. "Who you working for? Gimme a name."

"I've been sending stuff in to an editor. Name is Bill Gardener."

"He pays you for this?"

"If he gets it approved, someone sends me a check."

"Why are you investigating these businesses?" said Antonio. "What the hell is it all about?"

Bruce shrugged. "As I understand it, they want an investigative piece on mob influence and finance in businesses north of Boston."

"That's so much bullshit," said Antonio. "That Downy broad gave you this information, her and Beckman. She gave you some stolen CDs, didn't she?"

Bruce shook his head. "Nobody gave me anything."

"You're friends; you and her and her squeeze."

"Yeah, but what I'm doing is an investigative piece for the Eagle."

"What kind of help is that Downy broad giving you? Telling you shit? Show you some CDs? What?"

"We talk about what I'm doing. But she hasn't given me anything."

"I don't believe you," said Antonio nodding at Nick.

Bruce tried to duck, but the fist hit him hard on the cheek. Then another came at him from the other side.

Antonio touched Nick on the shoulder. "I think we have his attention."

They watched as Bruce slowly sat up. Blood ran from his nose and the corner of his mouth.

Bruce rubbed his bruised face and wiped away tears. "Fuckin' bastards," he moaned.

Antonio moved to stand in front of Bruce. He crossed his arms over his chest. "I want the CDs."

"I don't have any CDs. You've got all I have."

"No. I want the source. Where is the source – the CDs?" insisted Antonio.

Bruce glared at Antonio. "What the hell CDs are you talking about? I don't have any, goddamn it."

"Let me at him," said Nick, moving next to Antonio.

Antonio pushed Nick back, and then stepped closer to Bruce. "We're gonna find those CDs. When we do, we'll be putting a real hurt on your friends. You can believe it."

"We don't have any of your CDs," Bruce grumbled.

"What'll we do with him?" asked Nick.

Antonio pulled several flex-ties from his pocket and handed them to Nick. "Tie Brucie to the dining table leg. It'll give us time to get outa here, before he can work himself loose."

Nick looked at Antonio. "That's it?"

"Do it."

Nick shrugged.

CHAPTER 20

It was 7:20 in the evening as Tim and Jennifer watched TV in his apartment.

"It'll be nice to have an evening to ourselves," said Jennifer.

Then Tim's cell phone buzzed.

"I guess I spoke to soon."

Tim put the phone to his ear. "Hey Bruce. What's happening?"

"I had a visit this afternoon by two goons that slapped me around and tossed my place."

"Holy shit. Are you okay?"

"I'll live, but my face is all lumpy and hurts. Bastards."

"Did you call the cops?

"No. Can you guys meet me at Leon's?"

"Yeah, sure."

"I'll be at Leon's."

"Yeah. We'll head right over."

Tim turned to Jennifer. "He got hurt."

She brought her hand to her mouth. Her eyes wide. "Who...who hurt him?"

Tim shrugged. "He said to meet him at Leon's. Sounded like they worked over his face some."

"It has to do with those CDs doesn't it?" said Jennifer.

"He didn't want to talk. But I bet he hurts pretty bad."

—

Agents Brian Ludlow and Grant Foster sat in a conference room with cell phone records and various papers and empty coffee cups spread over the table.

"Hey Brian, look at this. Just this past month I have Downy making calls to banks all over the country, calls to Nevada Enterprises, several investment companies and lots of calls to Cipriano Enterprises."

"I sure wish we could have heard some of those."

"Yeah, there's also some calls to phones at Ocean Tower and several calls to Wilson Property Development in Burlington, Mass."

"Bastard's been busy. What have you got on Edward Owens?"

"Well, our boy Ed made eight calls to Sunset Travel and six calls to Eastland Bank, both in Boston," said Grant. "Also, we got several calls to the Miami Trade and Commerce Bank, and some to his home phone."

"What the hell was he up to?"

"That's what we have to find out."

—

When Tim and Jennifer entered Leon's Diner, they spotted Bruce in a corner booth. They sat down facing him.

Jennifer gasped. "Oh my god, your face!"

"Bruce, you didn't call the cops?"

"No. I couldn't identify them. Of course, they were Cipriano goons, who else." Bruce shook his head and reached for his coffee. "And I didn't want to have to expose all we're working on to the local cops. Screw it."

"Bruce, this is terrible. I'm sorry." Jennifer's eyes filled.

"Tell us what happened," said Tim.

"They were in my apartment waiting for me. They had tossed the place and didn't find what they were looking for."

"The CDs?" said Jennifer.

Bruce nodded. "They kept hitting me and I kept denying I even new what they were talking about."

"Christ…" muttered Tim.

"They forced me to unlock my computer and they copied off a bunch of stuff onto a thumb drive. Then they turned my briefcase upside down and emptied it onto the floor. They found the thumb drive I had with all the info on it. They copied that and then kept it."

"So, they have all that you were working on?" Tim stared at Bruce wide-eyed. "Everything?"

Bruce tried to smile. "I have my master copy on a thumb drive hidden in my car."

"But they now know what we know?" asked Jennifer.

Bruce nodded. "Basically."

Jennifer shook her head and wiped at her eyes with her hands. "I'm afraid of what Downy or Cipriano might do to both of you. They aren't going to let their business come unraveled…they won't. Those guys know we have the two CDs they were looking for and as long as they don't have them we're a threat to them."

Tim turned to her. "We don't know what they are going to do. I think its Bruce and I that are going to be the ones they come after." He turned to Bruce. "Do we dare go to the cops with what we have?"

"Look, we started out by Jennifer wanting to know who murdered Edward Owens. We still don't know. In the meantime, we got possession of the two CDs that expose the inner workings of the Downy – Cipriano empire. So now we're left with a ticking time bomb and we still don't have an answer to Jennifer's question."

"But what should we do?" asked Tim.

"I don't want to bring anymore attention to Jennifer. However, I have the makings of a great piece for the Eagle. They, or someone else, would pay big bucks for it. I think I should play out the cards dealt us and get as strong a hand as possible before we get called on it. What do you guys think?"

"Okay," said Jennifer, "but what do you want to do?"

"Tomorrow, I want to go to Ocean Tower and try to get an interview with the building manager to find out what businesses are operating there or is it just a parking spot for some of Cipriano's investments."

"I'll go with you," said Tim. "I'll put on a tie and blazer and be an extra pair of ears and eyes."

"How about me?" asked Jennifer.

"I think it would be safest for you if you stayed at your parent's place. You have both our cell phone numbers. It shouldn't take Bruce and me very long to get a meeting with the building manager. And if we don't get a meeting, we'll come right back."

—

Angelo sat in front of Frank Cipriano's desk explaining the recent events at Bruce Engelmann's apartment.

Frank slammed his fist down hard on his desk. "What the hell you telling me? He had all this on his computer? You shittin' me?"

Angelo placed the thumb drive on Frank's desk. "It's all on there, everything the bastard knows about us. Someone had to give him this info or he saw the missing CDs. How the hell else would the little prick know so much?"

"I agree with you. This is serious shit. What the hell did the bastard plan to do with this stuff? Go to the feds?"

Angelo shook his head. "I'm thinking he would likely go to the fuckin' newspaper. He said he sells his articles to the Eagle mainly."

"God damn it! This gets out there and our whole business comes unraveled. All this because of that weasel Owens? Son-of-a-bitch!"

"Can we put a stop to it, Frank? What do you want me to do?"

Frank was quiet for a few moments and then slowly shook his head. "We may already be too late. God damn that bastard!"

"I could take him out today. No problem. Take out his side kick too."

"No. This shit gets out; a hit on those guys would come back to us. No. Tell you what. You get a hold of that asshole Downy and bring him here…now."

"You got it."

—

Angelo knocked on Cipriano's office door and then pushed the door open. Downy entered the office and Frank gestured for him to sit down in front of the desk. Angelo remained standing, taking a stance behind Downy.

Frank told Downy of what Angelo discovered at Bruce's apartment.

"Do you realize the position we all are in now? Do you?" yelled Frank.

"Frank, I…"

"Shut up!" Frank took a breath. "This all started with you…you having this Owens guy killed."

"I didn't want him killed. I wanted the briefcase. I…"

"Shut up! You didn't even know what was going on in your own office… Owens socking away money, making the CDs…four of them…stealing secrets. This is all on you, you goddamn moron. Now we are in serious danger of coming unraveled…Century Design and us. The state and feds get a hold of this compilation put together by that reporter asshole, then we all are facing serious time in the joint."

"Frank, I'll get a hold of…"

"Shut the hell up!"

Downy looked down at his lap.

"This could open the door to an investigation of the Owens shooting. If you had your shit together you could have used non-lethal methods to bring Owens back in the fold. But no, you had your head up your ass and it's come to this." Frank paused for a moment. I have my suspicions about you and Owens' wife. Good bet her husband found out and stirred up this bucket of shit. You are one stupid bastard."

"Frank, let me explain…"

Frank looked at Angelo. "Get him the hell out of here."

CHAPTER 21

Bruce picked up Tim in his car mid morning and they headed to Ocean Tower in Salem, MA. They planned to try and interview someone there so they could learn more on the operation of the businesses in the building. They were going to attempt to reach the building manager or maintenance people; but failing that, they would try to get into the lobby and wait there for someone to show up.

They parked near the building, noticing few cars nearby. A notice on the door indicated the building was now configured for entry only with a key card. A wall-mounted phone was to be used by visitors to call the desired business to gain entry. There was no guard station or receptionist. There was a listing of businesses under glass on a wall by the phone with the respective phone numbers. Looking through the glass doors revealed an empty lobby except for two sofas and three stuffed chairs and a large round polished wood table with a phone and a large marble ashtray.

Tim read through the phone listing but did not recognize any business. Bruce dialed the phone number for several offices at random but did not get a response. Unable to gain entry, they decided to sit on one of the wooden benches by the door in hopes of being able to get someone to interview. They didn't have long to wait.

As a car drove up and parked nearby, Tim and Bruce readied themselves to address whoever came to the door. A well-dressed man of middle age approached the glass doors with a key card in his right hand and a briefcase in his left. Bruce and Tim stood as he came close.

"Excuse me, sir," started Bruce. "We're trying to contact the Business Office. Can you help us out?"

The man turned his head only slightly to acknowledge them. He shook his head. "Sorry. I can't help you."

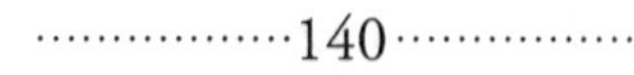

Tim and Bruce watched as the well-dressed man activated the door lock and entered the building. They watched him disappear into an elevator.

"I can read the elevator numbers," said Bruce. "Look, it stopped at the 9th floor."

Tim looked at the directory by the phone. "Turner Enterprises. Whatever that is."

"I'll do an Internet search later on these company names," said Bruce. "See if they're real."

"Let me call some of these numbers," said Tim. However, every number called had a recording asking the caller to leave a message.

An hour later no one had arrived and no on had left the building.

"Let's give it up for now," said Tim.

"Okay. I'll go home and look up all these names on the Internet. There is something really phony about this place. I have to wonder if there is anybody working here."

"Let's go home."

—

Robert Downy sat back in his chair and stared out the office window. Angst had been building up following his session with Cipriano. He began to suspect everyone of plotting against him. What exactly was Mario Russo doing at Century Design? There was never anything on his desk except his laptop computer. Downy felt uneasy; he had never asked Russo to do anything, and yet it seemed like the man was always busy. What had Cipriano asked him to do? Whatever it was, it hadn't been shared with him. Hell, wasn't he the manager of this company? Was Cipriano thinking of getting rid of him and putting in Russo – his own man to run the organization?

Downy worried that Russo had been installed in Century Design by Cipriano to gather evidence of malfeasance in the company's affairs. Downy feared Cipriano had in some way figured out that he was skimming from the accounts. Even if Russo couldn't prove this, it might be enough to have

Cipriano think twice about Downy's value to Century and make certain adjustments; adjustments that could include his demise.

He continued to stare out the window as he pondered the threatening situation. Downy was sure he had hidden his tracks well and the company's operations were designed to thwart investigations and audits by annoying governmental organizations. But still, if Cipriano convinced himself that Downy was skimming from the company, there would be no retirement in the Caribbean with Diane. It seemed to him, in order to remove the threat, he had to remove Russo. Sure, he thought, Cipriano would install someone else to audit the finances; still, it would give him time to work out a plan. But how to rid himself of Russo? Make it look like a random killing or an attempted car jacking, or maybe a poisoning? Whatever he did, it couldn't direct attention to him. He mused how he had been successful in the past; but that had been before the arrival of Cipriano into his life.

The following day Downy overheard Russo on the phone with Cipriano discussing what sounded like the development of a financial model for Ocean Tower. Russo seemed to be responding to questions from Cipriano regarding what seemed to him to be an empty building. Downy stood close to Russo's office cubicle and strained to hear his comments. Finally, Russo agreed to go to Ocean Tower in the next couple days to begin developing a financial model that would facilitate the Cipriano organization increased ability to manage customer monies. Having heard enough, Downy moved away from Russo's cubicle and back to his office. Why had Cipriano directed Russo to develop a financial plan for Ocean Tower? Was it because Cipriano had expected Downy to have already made such a plan, and he hadn't? Or had Cipriano and Russo discovered he had been skimming monies from the organization? Either way, he'd have to get rid of Russo and soon. Maybe then he would be better able to cover his tracks.

—

The next day after Cipriano had calmed down from the initial fury at Downy, he held a meeting with Downy and Angelo regarding the missing CDs and their importance to the organization. More to the point was what to do about it. Robert Downy and Angelo Costello favored using physical intimidation to bring Bruce, Tim and Jennifer into line. Cipriano listened to the arguments and then shook his head.

"Rough stuff will get the cops involved. That kind of visibility I don't need."

When Angelo started to argue, Cipriano raised a hand. "No. We know they have the information and probably the CDs. That newspaper guy – what's his name – he'll be feeding the story to the Eagle if he hasn't already. That's going to scare off investors and raise the interest of the FBI, at a minimum. I want to limit my exposure and the exposure of Century Design. We've got a good thing going here to launder our funds. It's not foolproof, but with careful management it can and has worked well."

Angelo tried again. "If we shut up the reporter then the other two will probably back off."

Downy shook his head. "I know her and she ain't one to give up."

Cipriano glared at Downy. "You had your accountant killed. That's what started this whole thing. You took it upon yourself to whack the guy. This whole mess is your doin'."

"He was spying, copying stuff to CDs," said Downy. "I had to stop him."

"Does it have anything to do with you poking his wife?" asked Cipriano in sarcasm.

Downy didn't reply, just shook his head.

"So, you had him killed. Now we have all kinds of attention on our business and ourselves and for what? The CDs and information is out there about to get in the papers. What the hell was accomplished?"

"We still need to get the CDs, don't we?" asked Angelo.

Cipriano looked at Angelo and nodded slowly several times. "You dress up and go find this Tim guy and make nice. Ask him to arrange for all three of them to meet with me to talk about this situation. No lawyers, just them and I here in my office, or any other quiet place. I want it done right away."

Angelo scowled. "Suppose they don't want to come...maybe afraid?"

Cipriano slapped his palm on the table. "You're gonna make nice and get them here. Now you two get the hell out and make it happen."

CHAPTER 22

Tim, Bruce and Jennifer were having lunch at Cory's Restaurant in Chelmsford. Tim looked up as a powerfully built man of almost six feet, clean-shaven and dressed in a blue blazer and khaki trousers approached their booth. "Can I help you?"

Angelo nodded. "Yeah. You can," He sat next to Bruce forcing him to slide over.

Bruce frowned. "Hey, do I know you?"

Angelo ignored the question and looked instead at Tim and Jennifer. "My boss is Mr. Cipriano."

Jennifer's eyes widened. Tim's jaw dropped. Bruce gasped, "What the hell is this?"

Angelo smiled. "Not to worry. Mr. Cipriano is concerned that we all got off on the wrong foot. He just wants to have a sit down with you folks and talk about things."

"That's so much bullshit," exclaimed Bruce.

Angelo turned toward him, still smiling. "Actually, Mr. Cipriano would like to talk to all three of you."

"Yeah, right." Bruce shook his head. "I know you, don't I?"

Again, Angelo ignored the question and looked at Tim and Jennifer. "Mr. Cipriano is a reasonable man. He would like to hear your concerns and issues since it doesn't seem like the current course of events is getting anyone anywhere."

"Don't listen to him," said Bruce.

"Where's this meeting supposed to take place?" asked Tim.

"It could be at his office in Woburn, unless you'd rather it be somewhere else."

Jennifer looked at Tim. "Not at his office."

"There's a popular Irish bar in Billerica. Nolan's Lounge," said Tim.

Angelo nodded. "I know where it is. Can't say I've ever been in it."

Bruce shook his head. "Don't go. This is ridiculous."

Tim looked at Jennifer. She nodded. He looked at Bruce. "We want to go. We'd like you to come with us."

"Big mistake," declared Bruce. "How can you trust him?"

"I don't, but this situation isn't good either. Will you come with us?"

Bruce scowled. "Can't let you two go by yourselves, that's for damn sure."

"Can we do this right away?" asked Angelo. "Drinks will be on me."

"Okay. We're just about done here."

Angelo took out his cellphone.

―

It was late morning when Russo called Cipriano. The task of getting a grip on the method and amount of skimming that he suspected Downy of performing over the last few years was turning out to be far more difficult than he had anticipated.

"Tony, I'm trying to tally up last months closings. However, my first pass shows that the total fund, after paying the dividends and accounting for all costs, is about two hundred grand short. And, that is just for the past month."

"Son of a bitch."

"Yeah. The difference *has* to come from the Cipriano account, otherwise we are back into a Ponzi situation," said Russo.

"Goddamn him."

"The investor's accounts are safe. They are solid. The dividends are being paid. So, when money is skimmed, or we have a down turn in investment income, the difference has to come from the Cipriano account. There is no place else."

"I understand that. We did it that way so we could keep the laundry machine running. I agreed to make up any losses. But this is outright robbery."

"I still don't have the particulars on how the sneaky bastard does it, but I'm working on it."

"Mario, I want to nail the prick, but I have to caution you. Downy is dangerous. Two partners died in his organization before I took control of it."

"I remember you telling me."

"I'm worried he may try something with you if he feels endangered."

"I'll stay alert. When are you getting a new director here? This guy has to go."

"I agree with you. Unfortunately, he is very good at his job. I want to keep you alive and put you in that chair when we wrap this up."

"Okay."

"Sorry, there's another call coming in that I better get. I'll get back to you." Cipriano pushed the button for the other line. "Cipriano."

"Angelo. Can you talk?"

"Yeah. Go ahead."

"I met up with the three characters we were talking about earlier."

"Oh? How did you make out?"

"Can you meet us at Nolan's Lounge in Billerica?"

"It's a fuckin' *Irish* bar."

"I know, but it's where they want to meet. They won't come to your office. We're all headed there now. Can you come right away?"

"Shit. Well, I guess I better, huh?"

"I'll have all three of them there."

"Okay. Give me a half hour."

"See you then."

Cipriano hung up and let out a long breath. He shook his head. "A goddamn Irish bar."

—

All three looked up as a well-dressed middle-aged man walked up to their booth. The man known to them as Angelo stood to one side.

"Folks, this is Mr. Cipriano," Angelo announced.

Looking at Bruce, Cipriano asked, "May I sit down?"

Bruce stared and then shrugged, and slid farther into the booth. He looked at Tim and Jennifer and rolled his eyes. Angelo grabbed a chair from a nearby table and sat at the end of the booth facing them. Cipriano looked from one to the other. No one had said a word.

A waiter appeared and took their drink orders. Jennifer, Tim and Bruce asked for beer. Cipriano requested double bourbon on the rocks. Angelo shook his head.

Cipriano grimaced. "I asked you all here as I think we got off on the wrong foot."

"I'll say," groused Bruce.

Cipriano turned to him with a steely look. "If you don't mind, I'd like to make some introductory remarks and *then* you all can jump in."

Bruce didn't respond.

"Century Design is an investment company that I control. I have a sizable stake in this company. All this may be old news to you but permit me to continue." Cipriano glanced at Jennifer. She bit her lip.

"Mr. Downy founded Century Design years ago establishing a financial environment intended to be lucrative to investors. Mr. Downy was making himself rich, while at the same time paying off investors. But, something had to give. On the latest economic downturn, he was unable to continue to pay his investors. It was at this time that I became aware of this situation and decided to buy into the company. This saved the investors, who didn't have a clue that anything was amiss. It also saved Mr. Downy from probable prison time."

The waitress brought the drinks and a moment passed as they sampled them.

Cipriano looked from Tim to Jennifer. "Are we good so far?"

Jennifer nodded. Bruce forced a yawn. Tim listened intently.

"I'm sure by now, since you've studied the CDs in your possession, you have concluded that Century Design is being used as a laundry for various Cipriano business interests. Although you think you have definite proof of this, I will continue to deny it and arrange my business at Century to make it impossible for anyone to state it as fact." He turned to look at Bruce. "Any attempt to publish accusatory stories based on what you saw on the CDs will be very painful for you. Am I getting through to you?"

Bruce scowled but nodded.

"Now we get down to the more immediate issue. When I took over the company Mr. Downy was kept on as Operations Manager since he was intimately knowledgeable of the operating methodology, something I had yet to fully grasp. Recently, however, it has become known to me that Mr. Downy has a get-rich agenda of his own."

Cipriano looked at Bruce. "This conversation is private and not for exploitation in the press or Internet or with any agencies. I will deny what I have said, but before that, there will be some effort made," he looked at Angelo, "to dissuade any of you from such hazardous behavior. I hope I have made myself understood."

Angelo sat stone-faced. Bruce didn't respond. Both Tim and Jennifer nodded. When Cipriano turned to look at Bruce again. Bruce nodded. "Yeah."

Jennifer raised her hand to her shoulder and looked at Cipriano.

Cipriano smiled. "Yes."

"I *saw* Mr. Owens get killed. It was a horrible thing that happened to that poor man. What did he ever do to deserve that? All this time I wanted someone to pay for what happened. It matters to me."

"I understand the killer met a bad end."

"Yes, but not the person *responsible* for what happened to Mr. Owens," said Jennifer.

Cipriano was quiet for a few seconds before responding. "Turning over rocks in this pursuit could result in one or all of you in serious harm. I have to caution you, the person or persons responsible for Mr. Owens demise will not abide by anyone exposing their culpability."

"Is that a threat to keep quiet?" asked Tim.

"Sounds like it to me," said Bruce.

"I think he's talking about Downy," said Jennifer.

"*I'm* not making any threats. There are others pulling the strings. I cannot do much about them, at least not yet."

"Well, what would you have me do?" asked Jennifer. "The murder of Mr. Owens is a real tragedy – the way he died. It upsets me to think about it. You won't tell me who orchestrated this?"

Cipriano shook his head. "I don't want to be responsible for any of you getting hurt or worse." He paused and looked at Jennifer. "I need some time to protect my organization. I *can* get you the satisfaction you're looking for. But, I need a little time."

Bruce looked at Cipriano. "You mentioned Mr. Downy had an agenda of his own. What would that be?"

"Mr. Downy has held a trusted position in the company. It made it easy for him to design methods and do things detrimental to Century Design and profitable for him."

"We're talking skimming, aren't we?"

"The scope of this is just now being assessed and understood. I would appreciate it if you all would allow me time to ferret out the details before you draw any conclusions or take any further actions in this regard," said Cipriano. "Can we agree on that?"

"And the person responsible for the murder of Mr. Owens? What about him?" insisted Jennifer.

Cipriano looked at her and nodded. "Give me some time and *I will* provide you with what you want to know."

Bruce shrugged. "I guess I'll water down the article I'm writing – for now."

"One other thing," said Cipriano looking from Jennifer to Tim. "Since you've got all the information you really need, I'd like to have the two CDs in your possession."

Jennifer looked at Bruce. "We don't need them anymore."

"You have them with you?"

"They've been in my purse since the first day." Jennifer grinned. "Safest place I could think of."

Bruce shook his head. "Might as well give them to him."

"You have to understand, I cannot allow any copies to surface anywhere. Do we understand each other on this?" said Cipriano.

"And we won't get bullied by your people anymore?"

"Agreed." Cipriano took the two CDs that Jennifer handed him.

No one said a word until Cipriano and Angelo had left the lounge.

"You guys believe him?" Bruce was agitated. "He can't believe we don't have copies. Why would he do anything he said?"

"At least now there's no reason for *his* goons to come after us," said Tim.

Bruce looked at Jennifer. "Did you get the idea that Downy is on a short string?"

"My ex-husband is a real dip-shit," said Jennifer, "but he's not stupid."

"He practically said Downy was responsible for Owens's death," said Tim. "Didn't you guys get that?"

"Yeah," Jennifer frowned.

"It wasn't all that subtle," said Tim.

"It isn't much of a stretch to believe he had Owens whacked to keep his own malfeasance from being discovered."

"I don't know about that. Could be Owens had his own thing going," said Bruce. "Anyhow, I do think Downy is on a short string and he probably knows it."

"He may be getting desperate," added Tim. "Maybe seeing *us* as a threat to him."

"I never believed he would hurt me," said Jennifer shaking her head. "But now I don't know. Maybe it was that I just didn't *want* to believe he had something to do with his partners dying."

Bruce scowled. "If Cipriano is worried that Downy is robbing him and could bring the whole organization down, why the heck doesn't he just get rid of him?"

"Kill him?" asked Tim.

"Yeah. Why keep him around?"

"He's the only one that really knows the nitty-gritty of how that organization works," said Jennifer. "He designed it."

Tim looked at Bruce. "Didn't you tell us the other day that Cipriano installed a guy in there, some kind of accountant, to get a grip on things? I bet he'll tell his boss what's going on pretty quick."

Bruce nodded. "Yeah. What's his name?" He scratched his head. "Russo. Mario Russo. I read the name in some financial paper."

Bruce looked at Jennifer. "Hey. Is Downy still getting it on with the widow?"

"The widow?"

"Yeah. The Owens widow," said Bruce. "I wonder if she thinks Downy ordered the hit on her husband?"

Jennifer shook her head. "I don't believe she does. Besides, we don't know it for sure…do we?"

"If she knew, would she tell the cops…tell someone?" asked Tim.

Jennifer shrugged. "I don't really know her. But, I just can't believe she'd keep a relationship with him if she knew."

"Unless she was in on it," Bruce commented.

"You talked to her. What do you think?" Tim glanced at Jennifer.

She shook her head slowly. "No, I don't think so. She referred to him as *her Edward*. That sounds like she cared something about him, even if she was cheating on him."

"I think we can safely assume Owens got hit on orders direct or indirect from Downy, and the job was done by one of Downy's associates and it had nothing to do with Cipriano." Bruce looked from Jennifer to Tim, "Right?"

They both nodded.

"But then, was it a Cipriano guy that whacked Downy's shooter?" asked Tim.

Bruce nodded. "Sure, on request of Jennifer's uncle. He's in tight with Cipriano."

Jennifer nodded. "I think so."

Bruce continued. "I think Downy is probably worrying about what Jennifer might tell a grand jury, if it came to that, and what this Russo guy would tell a grand jury. Also, we can't forget the Owens widow; she might have a lot to say, too."

Tim nodded. "If the FBI gets wind of what he's up to and starts rattling his cage, he's gonna be worried about the trouble Jennifer could make for him."

"He would hurt me?" she asked.

"I'd be worried," said Bruce.

CHAPTER

23

The phone on Frank Cipriano's desk buzzed. "Yes?"

"Mario Russo is on line two."

"Thank you." Frank pressed the button to connect. "Hey Mario. Where are you?"

"I'm at Ocean Tower going through the computer files that Downey has."

"For Ocean Tower or Century Design?"

"At the moment, Ocean Tower. Century is a whole different can of worms."

"Mario, call me back on the scrambler. Use code-three."

"Okay. Be a minute."

Frank put the phone back in the cradle. He knew Mario did not have any good news. His own suspicions had been growing over the past months, and now Mario was confirming that Downy was skimming accounts at both places.

When the scrambled-line indicator lit up, Frank picked up the phone and pressed the line button. "Mario? What do you have for me?"

"Frank, this is preliminary. However, it looks like the money paid for suites in this building as rent partially ends up in a separate account accessible only by Downy. The money going into the company fund seems much smaller than what I expect. I can't get into the account as Downy has it locked up, at least not yet. I wouldn't be surprised though, if the funds he's skimming doesn't stay in that account very long."

"And goes where?"

"That's the thing. I don't know. Funds can be transferred anywhere, and probably offshore. It could happen very quickly."

"The bastard is probably doing the same thing at Century Design."

"I'm sure he is," said Mario. "I just haven't got the proof yet. As you know, the system was set up to make auditing a near impossibility. He's taking advantage of this to skim off who knows how much."

"But you know he is, right?"

"Yeah. Things aren't adding up. We're talking maybe ten or twenty large every month."

"You shittin' me? How long has he been doing this?"

"Don't know. These are preliminary findings. I have a lot more work to do."

"I'm going to have Roy Wilson get his nose into this before I do anything else. I want to know the extent of it, who's all involved, and where the money is being stashed. Mario, you keep doing what you're doing and keep your files secure…and thanks."

"Okay. I'll be in touch."

——

Roy Wilson had long suspected what Frank had told him was true. He'd always thought of Robert Downy as a dangerous, dishonest and foolish man, not above ruining someone or causing them to disappear to further his ends. The early history of Century Design, founded by Downy, had been fraught with scandal and suspicious disappearances. Downy's fraudulent management of investor monies had brought him to the brink of ruin. The situation had caught the attention of Frank Cipriano, eager to develop a more robust means of laundering his steady income. He arranged to underwrite the operation, but kept Downy as chief of operations, justified by his intimate knowledge of the investors and instruments. It appeared now, however, that things were unraveling.

The murder of Edward Owens, thought Roy, had begun the unraveling of the organization. He was certain the murder had been orchestrated by

Downy and then carried out by a rather inept shooter. He was sure the killing had been done to prevent Owens from divulging secrets of how Downy was skimming off funds, funds that would eventually have to be made up by Cipriano to keep the investor accounts solvent. He knew that if ever an investor were late in receiving scheduled dividends, it would likely precipitate a visit by the SEC and FBI, with RICO charges a reality. At all costs, this couldn't be allowed to happen, and Cipriano had made *him, Roy Wilson,* point man to remedy the situation uncovered by Mario Russo.

Cipriano had valued Downy for his ability to attract investors and organize the company. However, his blatant thievery, the murder of Owens, and who knew what else, was forcing Cipriano to reevaluate Downy's worth. It was time to see what Downy was up to, and to get rid of him if need be.

Cipriano had told Roy that Russo had discovered Downy was skimming from the new venture at Ocean Towers. Cipriano was incensed at the betrayal and fearful of losing control to where the feds would be investigating. Roy knew this couldn't be allowed to happen.

Roy thumbed through his old Rolodex until he came to Surety Investigations. He and Mark Higgins had done business together in the early years. He had gone on to found an investigative service specializing in due diligence and covert financial investigations. Roy had no doubt Higgins could ferret out the devious doings of someone like Downy.

Roy picked up the phone on the second ring. "Hello Roy, Mark here."

"Hey. Tell me you have something. Remember this phone isn't very safe."

"I made some interesting discoveries; nothing the government doesn't know, I'm sure."

"Hope so. I'm getting some pressure on this, as you can imagine."

"First of all, Downy has six figure accounts in both Nicaragua and Panama."

"Jesus. You kidding? Six figures?" exclaimed Roy.

"That's what I'm told," replied Mark. "There's 368-large in one account and over 300 in the other."

"What you're *told*? Mark, I need tangible proof. This is serious."

"This guy I've been in contact with is fearful. He doesn't want to lose his job…or maybe worse. Can you free up some cash for me?"

"How much are we talking?"

"I think several thousand on each account might do it."

"Yeah, sure. That's not a problem. But I have to have tangible proof, stuff that can be verified. Not some phony forms made on a computer by this guy."

"I know my job, Roy."

"I know you do. I'm just saying…"

"There's more to this," said Mark.

"Okay…"

"Is the name Owens import to you?"

"Owens? Yeah, damn right."

"The name Diane Owens appears along with Downy as signatory to both accounts."

"You shittin' me? Diane Owens?"

"Yep. But there hasn't been any account activity by her…no one but Downy. Who is she?"

"Goddamn. She's the wife of the accountant that was killed. I told you…"

"Yeah, yeah. I remember. This guy Downy and her…what's the deal?"

"Mark, I have to get tangible proof of all this. You do what you have to do but get it to me."

"Okay. I hear you. I'll be in touch."

Roy hung up. "Diane Owens? That son-of-a-bitch!"

CHAPTER 24

Robert Downy led a trio of FBI agents into the conference room and closed the door. The agents were seated on one side of the long table and Downy on the other. He had decided at the last minute not to have any of his staff with him, as he didn't know in what direction the interview would go, and some things he as soon no one else heard about. He opened a leather folder to a blank page, and then sat back in the leather chair and smiled. "How can I be of help? Do I need a lawyer?"

The oldest of the three agents, sitting between the other two, opened his notebook. "I'm Special Agent Walter Barrow. To my right is Agent Glenn Foster. To my left is Agent Brian Nedham. We're conducting an investigation into the influence of organized crime in several financial institutions in eastern Massachusetts. You are free to stop this meeting at any time."

Downy cleared his throat. "Are there specific charges being brought against Century Design or Ocean Tower, or is this some sort of fishing expedition?"

"We understand the Cipriano Group is a major investor in Century Design," said Agent Barrow.

Downy nodded. "They are one of our many investors; but yes, probably the largest."

"The Cipriano Group is a front for the Frank Cipriano organized crime organization. It is the means by which they launder money."

"They have an investment account with Century Design. They electronically transfer funds in and out of their account as they wish."

"No doubt, each transaction is under $10,000?"

Downy shrugged. "Probably."

"And of course, you send in the required IRS forms."

"That's what the accountants get paid to do."

Agent Barrow grinned. "Of course." He then turned to his right. "Glenn?"

Agent Glenn Foster looked at Downy. "How is the management of Century Design set up? What role does Cipriano have in the management of the company?"

Downy returned the gaze. "As you must know, Century Design is a private company. There are no public officers. That said; I am always open to advice and suggestion from our larger investors. Their experience and wisdom are a valuable resource."

"So, you are the sole manager of this company. It is you that decides the investments to be pursued so to be able to provide the investors with the promised returns of two points above the general market."

Downy smiled and rolled his pen back and forth on the page. "I listen to advice from my accountants, as well as constantly investigating investment opportunities so as to be able to stay ahead of the general market. But yes, I do make the final decisions on investment strategy."

"So, if Cipriano *suggests* a certain investment, you would be inclined to consider it."

"Of course, I would investigate it as I would any opportunity. I would need to assess the soundness, the history, the business model, and so forth.

"Due Diligence."

"Exactly."

"Wasn't Century Design in financial difficulties some years ago and Cipriano came to the rescue with a huge influx of money?" asked Agent Foster.

"We had a rough period. It was tough going."

"And Cipriano came to the rescue?"

"He started a major account with us. It helped considerably in getting us back on track."

"He exercises special privileges, I imagine, after such an investment."

Downy shrugged. "His account earns interest like everyone else's."

"Since all of the investor accounts earn about two points above market, isn't it true that in a soft economic period Cipriano may realize less than the other accounts?"

The three agents stared at Downy.

"It varies. Some years Cipriano might earn more or even less than the regular accounts."

"Why would that be?" asked Agent Foster. "Something different about that account?"

Downy felt the pressure but had steeled himself for this inevitability. Were they after him or Cipriano? Maybe both? "Well, when Cipriano opened the account that helped us get back on our feet, we didn't guarantee him two points like the other accounts. We allowed the return to his account to float so some years he realizes maybe ten percent and some years there might be a loss of a point or two."

Agent Foster shook his head. "And you've always made the interest payment to every investor?"

"Absolutely. No one has ever lodged a complaint."

"Has the SEC examined your methods and accounts?"

Downy shook his head. "They had no reason to."

Special Agent Walter Barrow looked to his left at Agent Brian Nedham. "You have some questions for Mr. Downy?"

"Yes," replied Nedham, "I do." He looked down at his open notebook and then up at Downy. "You were married to Jennifer Wilson for a few years while she was employed at Century Design."

Downy nodded. "Yes."

"What was her role during her employment there?"

"Jennifer had minor accounting duties, mostly bookkeeping."

"She had been married to you. Did she not have managerial responsibilities as well?"

Downy shook his head. "Not really. She may have *thought* she had," he smiled, "but she didn't."

Downy realized Jennifer could tell the FBI enough to have him indicted, if not convicted, in the financial dealings with the Cipriano organization. He felt, with her intimate knowledge of the company, as well as of himself, she was more of a threat than Mario Russo. Downy hoped the interview would be over soon, as he had to get some antacids, his stomach was churning.

"Mr. Downy, you had another bookkeeper employed at Century Design until of late, a Diane Owens. Did you not?"

Downy nodded. *Where are these bastards going with all this?* "Yes. She quit some months ago."

"Before her husband was killed?"

"I, uh, yes. Edward Owens was my primary accountant and a very able employee. I sorely miss him."

"What role did Diane or Edward Owens have in the management of the company?"

"Diane had no managerial duties at all. Edward, being my primary accountant, kept me informed of investments that weren't performing and made suggestions to improve overall company earnings."

"What sort of personal relationship did you have with Diane Owens?"

"I met with the Owens' socially from time to time. We went to dinner and enjoyed ourselves at different clubs." Downy didn't like the direction of the questioning. He had to be careful. His stomach hurt.

Agent Nedham looked at his notes and then back up at Downy. "It seems that you had a more serious relationship with Diane Owens since her husband was killed, if not before that."

Downy shook his head. "I met with her a few times to advice her on financial matters after the death of her husband."

Bile tried to come up his throat as the FBI pressed their questions. Both Diane and Jennifer could bring the whole operation down on his head, as well as on Cipriano.

Agent Nedham then switched his attention to Mario Russo. "What duties does Mr. Russo perform at the company?"

Downy shrugged. "Russo is an auditor assigned by the principal investor to make sure everything is okay."

"So, he's not from one of the major auditing firms?"

Downy shook his head.

"An auditor assigned by Cipriano?"

"Yes. We agreed to have Russo make the audit. As the major account holder, I couldn't refuse."

"Really?"

Downy nodded. "He *is* the major account holder."

Special Agent Walter Barrow closed his notebook and the meeting drew to an end. "Mr. Downy, it is likely a grand jury will be impaneled to investigate Cipriano influence in various financial institutions."

"What kind of influence?"

Agent Barrow smiled but didn't reply.

Downy frowned. "When is this supposed to happen?"

"You can expect it in the next 60-90 days."

The agents stood up, picked up their notebooks, and looked at Downy.

"I'll walk you to the door." Downy left the room behind the group, his stomach in distress.

When the agents left the building, Downy fumbled in his pocket for a roll of antacid tablets. As he chewed two of them he thought of the trouble he could be in. Downy suspected Jennifer would be ratting on him and knew her testimony could put him away for years. He also knew that Russo would be able to seriously damage him with the results of his audit, unless he was stopped. He surmised if either of them testified it would result in his indictment and a hefty prison sentence. He also considered that Cipriano might have him killed to keep him from implicating Cipriano in any illegal activities. What troubled Downy now was what would happen when the FBI put pressure on Diane. She didn't know about, and hadn't participated in, all of Downy's history; so how would she react when she heard all the FBI had to tell her?

—

The next day Special Agent Walter Barrow visited Roy Wilson at his condo/office in Burlington to inquire about his relationship with Century Design and more specifically with Robert Downy.

"I'm hoping you can help us on a matter. Of course, you can stop this any time."

"Although I know of Downy," said Wilson, "I have no relationship with Century Design or Ocean Tower. Robert Downy is the owner and Chief Operating Officer of the company. I have not been involved with that company in any capacity."

"How then do you know Mr. Downy?" asked Barrow.

"I am the uncle of his ex wife, Jennifer Wilson. Her father is my brother. He and his wife are currently on vacation in Europe."

"With Downy's ex wife as your niece, I have to assume you have a good understanding of the Century Design organization." Agent Barrow looked steadily at Wilson.

"I saw my niece several times a year at some function or other, but as to the organization of Century, I don't think she was privy to much. Leastwise, I never heard much about it."

Agent Barrow turned to a different page of his notebook and looked up. "I understand you have been paid for work performed for the Cipriano organization. Do I have that right?"

Wilson nodded. "On several occasions I have been asked to consult on real estate investment opportunities they were considering. The work was done on an hourly consulting basis and billed that way."

"Can you clarify the type of consulting you provided?"

"I am very familiar with the commercial real estate markets in Florida and Las Vegas. We are developing office buildings in these areas. Thus, it is natural for Cipriano to ask me to consult with them on investment possibilities in those locations."

"And Cipriano leases office space from your company?" asked Barrow.

"I don't think so. In any case the actual leasing is managed by different companies we contract with."

"So, you're not sure?"

"I'm not sure, but I don't think so."

"Is Cipriano a direct investor in your company?"

Wilson shook his head. "No. Wilson Development is a privately held company."

"Your capitalization came from where?"

"The Wilson family has been invested in real estate here in the US and in Europe for many decades. Funding the start of Wilson Development didn't require outside resources."

"How much are you invested in Century Design and Ocean Tower?"

"We are not invested at all in either place."

"What do you know about Century Design and Ocean Tower? What kind of company is it?"

Wilson shrugged. "I understand that Century Design is an investment company, mainly for high rollers. Ocean Tower is an office building that leases suites to different commercial tenants. I've never been in either building."

"It's all one company though?"

"Yes. Century and Ocean are the same company and is operated by Robert Downy."

After a brief break to refill coffee cups and grab a donut, the meeting continued with Agent Barrow bringing the focus back to Cipriano.

"What's the nature of your personal relationship with Frank Cipriano?"

"I've known Frank for about ten years. We met at a real estate forum in Miami Beach. Since then, I've often advised Frank on investment opportunities both formally and informally in the Florida and Las Vegas markets."

"Does Cipriano move any monies through Wilson Development into accounts off shore?"

Wilson shook his head. "I've never done that for Cipriano or for anyone else."

"Do you also give financial advice to Robert Downy?"

"No. I've not done business with Downy." He didn't elaborate.

Agent Barrow advised Wilson a grand jury would likely be impaneled within a few months to explore Cipriano influence in some financial institutions, and that he would be asked to testify to what he knew of companies like Century Design. Wilson nodded his understanding.

When the FBI agent left his office, Roy Wilson realized how much more complicated and potentially dangerous his situation had become. He would have to talk to Cipriano without being observed or overheard. He worried, if the FBI came down hard on Downy, Cipriano could be 'thrown under the bus.' Since with this thought, Downy must now suspect he might not live to see the grand jury, mused Wilson.

—

A day later Special Agent Walter Barrow and Agent Sandra Martin walked up to the home of Diane Owens and knocked on the door. They had come unannounced in hope Diane had not been forewarned of the FBI interest in Downy and Cipriano. The door opened to an attractive middle-aged woman. The agents displayed their identification as Agent Barrow made the introductions.

"Mrs. Diane Owens?"

She nodded. "Yes?"

"This is FBI Agent Sandra Martin and I am Special Agent Walter Barrow."

Diane exhibited little interest, but stood aside inviting them in. "Have a seat, please. What can I do for the FBI?"

"We would like to clear up some things we're looking into. Of course, you may stop this meeting at any time. We're part of an investigation into the influence of organized crime in some financial institutions in eastern Massachusetts."

Diane looked composed and at ease. "What does that have to do with me?"

Agent Barrow opened his notebook, glanced at the page, and then looked at Diane. "We understand you were employed at Century Design for a few years. What were your responsibilities?"

"I was hired as a book keeper."

"You had no managerial responsibilities?"

She shook her head. "Spreadsheets. Lots of spreadsheets."

"You were married to Edward Owens at that time?"

"Yes. We'd been married for six years. He was murdered."

Both agents looked at Diane. "We're sorry for your loss," said Barrow. "Have the authorities determined what happened?"

"Not to my satisfaction. It turns out both my husband and his killer were assassinated." Diane shook her head and scowled. "I've never received a sensible report from the police; still under investigation according to them."

Agent Martin looked at Diane. "You should have heard by now, I would think."

Diane shrugged. "You would think…"

"How well did you know Mr. Downy?" asked Agent Barrow.

"I saw him every day. I reported to Edward, my late husband. Mr. Downy was his boss."

"Did you see each other socially?"

"Sure. There were dinners and club nights every now and then."

"You left the company before your husband was killed."

Diane nodded. "Several months before." She squirmed in her seat and rearranged her skirt. "What's all this have to do with organized crime?"

"Please bear with us for a few more minutes," said Agent Barrow. "Has Mr. Cipriano been a frequent visitor to Mr. Downy at Century Design?"

"Frequent? No. Maybe every six months or so."

"Do you participate in those meetings?"

Diane shook her head. "Hardly. I do spread sheets."

"Are you aware of the accounts that Cipriano has at Century?"

"No. The accounts are identified to me only as numbers. That's what goes into the spreadsheets."

"You've been away from Century for a while. Do you still see Mr. Downy?" asked Agent Martin.

Diane's gaze shifted to a spot on the wall just past where the agents sat. "Since my Edward was killed, Mr. Downy has been helpful in advising me on financial matters. I've seen him several times, trying to get my things in order."

"Not socially?"

Diane didn't meet her gaze. "Well, we do spend several hours at a time discussing how best to handle my finances. I'm not very knowledgeable about those things."

"Mrs. Owens, what was your husband doing in the shopping mall on that fateful day?" asked Agent Barrow.

She grimaced and shook her head. "I don't know. No one can tell me."

Agent Barrow stood up and Agent Martin followed suit. "We apologize for taking up your time," said agent Barrow. "You've been very helpful."

—

It had been over a day since Tim heard from Jennifer. He had called Bruce Engelman, but he hadn't heard from her either.

"I just don't understand it," said Tim on the phone with Bruce. "Where could she be? Has something happened to her? I've called her cell phone at all hours and left messages. I called over to her parent's place. I even called Downy's office at Century and Roy Wilson, but they haven't heard from her either."

"You should call the cops," said Bruce. "She's an adult, so I don't think the police will be very helpful. But you need to make out a report on her being missing."

"Yeah. I'll do that. Something is wrong here. I'm really worried."

"Keep me posted."

"I'll call you later." Tim closed his phone. He was startled by a sharp knock at the door.

Tim yanked the door open, hopeful that it was Jennifer. Instead, he stared at two FBI IDs.

"I'm Special Agent Barrow and this is Agent Brian Nedham."

Hadn't he seen Nedham before, he wondered? "FBI. What's up?"

"May we have a few minutes of your time?" asked Agent Barrow.

Tim opened the door wide. "Sounds like I should call my lawyer."

"This won't take long. You can stop at any time.'

"Alright. Come on in. Have a seat."

The two agents sat down on the couch and opened their notebooks.

"What can I do for you?" asked Tim.

Agent Barrow glanced at his notes. "We're part of a team investigating the influence of organized crime in several financial institutions in New England."

"I don't know from finance, barely able to balance my checkbook"

"Please bear with us. I think you can be of help."

Tim shrugged. "Okay."

"How acquainted are you with the people and operation of Century Design?"

"I never heard of it until a few months ago."

"When you met Jennifer Wilson?"

"Yes."

"You and Jennifer were present when Mr. Owens was murdered in the mall?"

"I did not witness it. I was on my way out."

"But Jennifer was a witness."

"That's what she said."

"And you met her…?"

"As she was leaving the mall. She was scared shitless at what she had seen. She asked me to walk her to her car."

"You had no idea who Mr. Owens was?"

"Not then. Later, Jennifer told me about him and the Century Design Company."

"She had been married to Mr. Downy at some point. He runs the company."

"That's what she said," replied Tim.

"How do you understand where Roy Wilson fits into the picture?" asked Agent Barrow.

"She told me he was her uncle. That he was big in the commercial real estate business in Miami and Las Vegas."

"And his connection to Century Design and Mr. Downy?"

Tim shook his head. "I don't know that there is one."

"How do you think the Cipriano organization is influencing Mr. Downy and Mr. Wilson?"

"I have no idea."

Agent Barrow smiled. "Really? Surely, Mr. Engelman has filled you in on these things. You and he are friends. Actually, you and he and Ms. Wilson are rather close now, aren't you?"

"Sure. We get together and talk about what's happening."

"What role, do you think, Cipriano plays in the operation of Mr. Downy's and Mr. Wilson's businesses?"

"I don't know."

Agent Barrow tilted his head. "I think you *could* be of some help here. You know Cipriano is a criminal organization, and he is a major investor in Century Design."

"But I don't know what *role* he has in Century."

"When you talk to Ms. Wilson, how does she describe the influence of Cipriano? Surely, she must have some opinions, having been part of Century and married to Downy."

"Other than stating Cipriano is the largest investment account, she doesn't know of any relationship Downy might have with Cipriano."

"And your friend, the reporter, he says the same thing?"

Tim shrugged. "He looks at Century with a more jaundiced eye, but then that's what he does with everything. He's a reporter."

"Have you talked with Jennifer Wilson in the last few days? We haven't been able to reach her."

Tim bit his lip. "I'm worried about her. I haven't been able to reach her the last day or so. I'm going to report her missing as soon as we're done here."

"Does she disappear from time to time? Go out of town?"

Tim shook his head. "Not since I've known her. I'm very worried."

"Has she been threatened?"

"She has been on edge ever since the shooting in the mall."

"Who does she blame for that? Downy? Cipriano? Someone else?"

"She doesn't know who is to blame, or why it happened. That she saw the incident makes her worry about repercussions."

"Do you think her disappearance is related to the incident?"

"I don't know. Are we done yet? I want to call the police about her."

"Sure. We'll let you make the call. Maybe we'll talk some more in a day or so." The two FBI agents stood up, shook hands with Tim, and left.

"Something hokey here," said Agent Nedham as he got in the car.

"You don't believe the missing woman story?" asked Special Agent Barrow.

"You know, that's the only part of his story I do believe. I think those three friends know way more than they're telling us. The thing is if Downy or Cipriano sees Jennifer Wilson as a potential witness that could incriminate them, then she may be in some real trouble."

"Well, so far, I think her uncle and the Owens woman are not a threat to Jennifer. But you're right, Cipriano and Downy certainly could be."

"Kinda odd that she would go missing just as this investigation is tightening around Downy and Cipriano," commented Nedham.

"Yeah, it is."

"Maybe the cops will get involved. It's been over 24 hours," said Nedham.

"We'll check around. After all, we *do* have her on our list to interview."

"Yep, we do."

CHAPTER 25

Downny looked at his watch as he walked to Jennifer's apartment. "10:48. Late. But, what the hell." He knocked firmly. "Come on, open the damn door." He heard a noise. Then the door opened against the safety bar.

"Rick, damn it, what are you doing here? It's really late."

"Please, I have to talk to you. Things are getting crazy. Diane is missing. Cops are asking questions. Please, let me in for a few minutes. I don't want to talk through the door."

"Just for a few minutes." Jennifer opened the door and Downy stepped in. She took a few steps back from him. "Now what the heck is so important that couldn't wait until tomorrow?"

Downy was perspiring. "Look, you must know…the cops, FBI are trying to find me, trying to hang some shit on me that your friends cooked up. They have Cipriano all pissed off. I don't know where Diane went…can't find her." He stopped and caught his breath.

"I don't know what the cops are doing. What do you want from me? Jesus, you're sweating."

He ran the back of his hand over his brow. "You gotta help me. There's going to be a grand jury. I just need to know that you'll back me up."

"Damn it, I'm not going to lie for you. I just won't."

"It's those asshole friends of yours, isn't it?" Downy's voice rose. "Those bastards started all this."

"No. It was you. What you had done to poor old Evans. That's what started all this. You!"

"You crazy bitch. I knew you'd screw me over." He reached into his jacket pocket. "Well, I'm not going to let you fry me." He pulled a stun gun from inside his jacket.

Jennifer took another step back. "What the hell is that? Get away from me!"

Downy quickly forced the stun gun against her neck and Jennifer dropped to the floor. He looked around the room and spotted the pull-cords on the Venetian blinds and groped for his pocketknife. Quickly he cut down some of the cords and bound Jennifer's ankles together and then tied her wrists together. In the kitchen he found a dry dishrag and fastened it over her mouth with another tie. He looked at his handy work and satisfied that Jennifer could breath through the porous rag, dragged her to the door.

He peeked from behind the blinds and saw that the neighborhood was quiet with hardly a window lit. Most people had to go to work in the morning. His car was only forty feet away. He should be able to carry her that far, he thought. He looked at her, noticing she was still out. He needed to do it now and quickly.

Downy turned the light off in the living room, leaving only a small lamp on in the dining area. He opened the door and looked at the neighborhood. It was quiet and dark; a streetlight was far down the street. He picked up Jennifer in both arms, struggled to get the door open, and stepped outside. Leaning Jennifer against the doorframe, Downy reached the doorknob and pulled it closed. Hefting Jennifer in his arms again, he moved quickly to his car.

He leaned Jennifer against the car as he opened the trunk. In a moment he had her dumped in there and the trunk lid closed. When he entered the car, he heard thumps coming from the trunk and knew Jennifer was now conscious. He decided to take a circuitous route to the seaside town of Beverly, hopefully without detection by police. He didn't want to kill Jennifer just then, but he knew he might have to if she became animated and likely to draw attention. His plan was to send her to 'live with the fishes.'

The bitch posed a real risk, thought Downy. Her knowledge of his business and what she knew about the death of earlier associates justified the action he had to take. And further more; her obsession with solving the mystery of old man Evans' demise with those asshole friends of hers would surely lead the authorities to his door, if not to a grand jury and prison. He didn't hate Jennifer, he thought, but he'd do what he had to do.

It was almost midnight when Downy arrived at Gateway Marina in Beverly. The place was dark with lighting only at the docks where several large motor-yachts were moored. The offices were dark. Downy stopped at the chain link gate and reached out and entered a code on the keypad. The gate rolled open and he drove into the yard. The gate closed behind him. He stopped for a minute and checked for anyone on the property or on one of the yachts. He saw nothing alarming. Downy drove past a luxury yacht to stop at a rundown pier where an old dilapidated cabin cruiser was moored. He turned off his headlights.

When he opened the trunk of the car, Jennifer tried to scream and kicked her bound legs at him in futile angry movements. Downy shook his head and then pressed the stun gun against her neck and she went quiet. He carried the limp form aboard the creaky boat and down into the hold. At the very front of the boat was a large cushioned bed. He tied her to an upright support member and left the cords on her hands and ankles. He checked her gag and decided to leave it. When she regained consciousness, she again tried to scream. He turned to her and said, "Relax. I'll turn you loose in a day or two. I'll have to tend to a couple things first." He knew however, she and his old boat would disappear in the sea in a day or so.

On leaving the forward room, Downy closed the door and wrapped part of a mooring rope through the handles until the door was tight and not movable. Without a backward look, he disembarked from the boat, got back in his car, and without his headlights drove to the office building and parked behind it. At the door to the building, he punched in a code to gain access.

—

Tim hurried into the Lowell Police Station to report Jennifer missing. The desk sergeant seemed less than persuaded by Tim's pleas. "She's missing. Something's happened to her. We need to find her. She's been gone over 24 hours. No one's seen her."

Tim was agitated and the bored sergeant raised his anxiety further. "Calm down. Fill this out and I'll start the process. However, this Jennifer is a grown woman. She can do what she wants."

Tim worked on the form. "Something's happened to her. She'd always call her friends if she could."

"You have a picture of this young lady?" The officer pursed his lips and waited for a reply.

Tim shook his head. "I don't have one on me."

"We could use a photo."

"Yeah. I'll have to find one. Can't you do something? She's in some kind of trouble."

The sergeant looked at him critically. "What kind of trouble would that be?"

"Her ex-husband…ex-employer… I think he's behind this. The guy is Richard Downy."

"Uh-huh. Where did I hear that name before?"

"He's being investigated…he's been linked to that shopping mall murder in Burlington."

"Really?" The sergeant wrote something on a notepad, and then looked up at Tim. "We'll get started as soon as the next shift starts. All the detectives are out right now. Give us a call tomorrow. Email us a photo."

Tim shook his head and left the building.

Tim kicked off his loafers when he entered his apartment. He was uncomfortable. His stomach was roiling and deodorant long since failed. He was certain Jennifer wouldn't disappear on her own without telling him why and to where. No, someone had grabbed her. It had to be Downy; it had to be. He sat down on the couch and looked at his phone. Then he took a deep breath and dialed Frank Cipriano's number.

"Hello. Cipriano."

"Mr. Cipriano, this Tim Beckman."

"You again? What's the problem?"

"Jennifer is missing. No one's seen her in over 36 hours. I'm worried sick something happened to her."

"This isn't the lost and found department."

"I'm sorry to bother you. I made a report with the Lowell police. I'm just sick with worry."

"Uh-huh. Just what do you think happened to her?"

"I tried calling Downy but can't get a hold of him. I keep thinking that she might pose the biggest risk for him if it comes to a grand jury. Frankly, I'm very scared something might happen to her."

"You mean Downy…that's what you mean. Right?"

"Yes. I can't locate him either. I was hoping you might know…"

"Christ, you're the bane of my existence. I'll see if I can get a hold of him and see what he knows."

"I appreciate anything you can do. I'm so afraid of what might happen to her."

"Yeah. Yeah. Later." Cipriano hung up.

CHAPTER 26

Russo had met with Frank Cipriano earlier that morning. Cipriano had wanted to make sure Russo knew of the interviews being held by the FBI with people from Century Design and Ocean Tower. The FBI focus was assumed to be on discovering what influence the Cipriano organization was exerting on the two businesses headed by Downy. Russo listened intently as Cipriano explained his concerns of what a grand jury investigation might reveal, specifically, the laundering of illicit monies from Cipriano Enterprises. Cipriano admitted he was too tightly linked to the purported misdeeds of Downy to escape scrutiny. He urged Russo to complete his 'audit' as soon as possible as he felt indictments were likely forthcoming.

When Mario Russo entered the Century Design building in early afternoon, he heard the worry and rumors from some of the accounting staff regarding the disappearance of Downy. No one had seen or heard from him in two days and attempts to reach his ex-wife, Jennifer, had been futile. Phone call memos had piled up on his desk. Russo agreed to have the calls routed to his phone so at least he could keep the essential business operations going. The rumors Russo heard suggested Downy was in hiding from FBI investigators and a possible grand jury summons.

Russo knew he too was in the same situation as Jennifer and could face the same dangers from Downy. In a grand jury investigation, he too would be required to tell all he knew about Century Design and Ocean Tower. Russo worried Downy would take steps to neutralize any threat.

Meantime, Russo continued to investigate the routing of investor's monies at Century Design. It became evident that commingling of investor funds with that of Cipriano Enterprises and their Las Vegas sources formed the basis of Downy's investment methods. Russo found that large blocks of monies were placed in risky financial instruments that paid well above average market returns. He worked to create a plan that would allow him to operate the company in a similar manner to that of Downy.

Russo hadn't talked to Cipriano about plans to remove Downy from the organization, as he really didn't want to know how that would happen. However, he had no doubt that Cipriano would not allow the chaos that threatened to derail the business and expose them to the severity of FBI and SEC scrutiny to continue. Russo had to develop plans quickly so when Downy was removed the business of the organization could continue successfully under new management installed by Cipriano, as Cipriano Enterprises was the underwriting organization for Century Design. The existing plans were evidently only in Downy's head, as Russo could find no meaningful documentation describing the structure or processes in any formal documents. Russo had been told to develop a management plan so even if Cipriano was jailed, the organization would continue as before with Russo presumably as head.

CHAPTER 27

Bruce and Tim were in Tim's apartment worrying about Jennifer's disappearance. Tim felt an increasing sense of dread as his chest tightened and a bead of sweat appeared on his brow. He had to find her; if something happened to her he wouldn't forgive himself. Tim had just finished calling everyone they knew that might have some idea where Jennifer might have gone. "I don't know who else to call."

"No one answers Downy's phone," said Bruce, looking at his phone.

"No one's seen him in two days." Tim shook his head. "This is bad; both of them gone. I am really scared now."

"That bastard Downy is up to something. The FBI is breathing down his neck and maybe there'll be a grand jury. He's got to be worried about what Jennifer could say because she'd be the first person they'd call."

"Yeah, no one knows more about him or the organization than Jennifer. I'm getting more panicked by the minute," said Tim. "She knows of all the sordid events back then. Especially, when two key investors met their end."

Bruce stood up and paced the floor and then went to stand at the window.

"Look, we can't just sit here," said Tim. "Downy is our best bet. We need to find the bastard and *force him* to tell us where he's taken her."

Bruce turned to Tim. "Okay, but I've called every place I can think of and can't find him. What have we missed?"

"You have his address? What does he drive?" asked Tim. "We have to start somewhere."

"I'm sure he's got a nice set of wheels in his garage at home, but all I've seen him with is an old gray Nissan."

"Since no one answers his damn phone," said Tim, "let's check out his place and make sure he's not there. If he's there, he's going to tell us where she is – one way or another."

Bruce was looking at his smart phone and nodding his head. "Hey, I got it here. He lives in a condo. Got the address."

"We're going right now." Tim stood up.

"Wait. Didn't you, or was it Jennifer, say that Downy had a boat at one time?" asked Bruce.

"Yeah, she told me that. You think…?"

"Could be. Where the hell would he keep it? I bet it isn't too far from Century or Ocean Tower."

"Beverly? It could be anchored right in Beverly," said Tim. "How do we find out?"

Bruce grinned. "I've got an idea. We go to his place and we park nearby where we can see that he isn't home. Then we walk over and break a window; maybe there's one at the front door. I'm sure a guy like him has the place wired like Fort Knox. Then we hustle back to the car and drive around until the cops come to check it out, and if we're lucky so will Downy. When the asshole goes into his condo, we go in right behind him."

"Yeah. He will tell us where she is or I'll redecorate his face."

"What'll we use for a weapon? I don't have a gun," said Bruce.

Tim frowned. "Neither do I."

"Think we can take him by surprise…and tie him up…electric cords maybe?"

"I've got a Leatherman in my pocket. You?"

"I've got a regular pocket knife," said Bruce.

"Can we take him…if we surprise him?" Tim sounded doubtful.

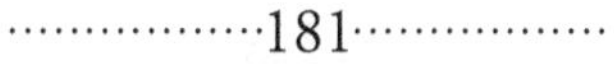

"He's bound to be armed. We *gotta* surprise him."

"We can't leave there until he tells us," Bruce insisted, "or shows us where she is."

Tim nodded. "He'll tell us. She better be okay or I'll kill him."

"Okay, lets go. We'll start at his house."

"We can't get caught…"

"We won't."

The ruse at Downy's condo worked as hoped. After breaking the window at the entrance doorway, Tim and Bruce drove around until they saw the police show up. Thirty-five minutes later they saw Downy drive up in his old Nissan. Downy and the police engaged in a conversation for five minutes and then the police left.

Tim parked his car behind the Nissan and not wasting a second, went with Bruce quickly to the side door where Downy had gone seconds earlier. They quickly opened their knives and gripped them tightly. Tim took a quick look through the door window and not seeing Downy, quietly opened the door. He whispered for Bruce to take a position that shielded him from the hallway and living area from where Downy would appear. Then, Tim gripped the knob and slammed the door closed.

In a few seconds Downy came around the corner from the living area and stared at Tim standing in the middle of the kitchen. "Who the fuck are you?" he yelled.

Bruce sprung at Downy as he came into the kitchen with his attention fixed on Tim. The knife blade jabbed into Downy's neck drawing blood. "Don't move, asshole."

"Hey! What the hell is this…fuckin' holdup?"

Tim moved to Downy and frisked him for a weapon. He shook his head, "Nothing. I'll get some wire."

"You two are dead meat," mumbled Downy. "Hey, don't I know you, asshole? You're gonna be dead."

Bruce pushed the blade deeper into Downy's neck. Blood oozed from the wound. "Shut the hell up."

"What…what you bastards want? My wallet is in my office…down the hall."

Tim returned with a long section of electrical cord. "Stereo don't work anymore."

"What the hell…?"

Tim tied Downy's arms and wrists together behind him. He pulled a kitchen chair to the middle of the room and forced Downy to sit. Bruce stood behind him, the knife jabbing Downy in the neck.

"Get that off of me, you bastard!"

Tim swung a closed fist back-handed across Downy's face. "Listen up. You want to keep living, you'll tell us exactly where we can find Jennifer."

"What? Who the hell are you two creeps?"

Bruce sliced across Downy's neck to produce more pain than bleeding. "Aren't you listening, asshole? He asked you where Jennifer was."

"Who the hell… You guys are gonna be dead meat."

Tim swung his fist back-handed into Downy's face. Blood and tears ran down his chin. "Answer me!"

Bruce made a long cut on the side of Downy's neck, going deeper than before. Blood seeped down his collar. "Stop, goddamn it!"

"Tell us. Where is Jennifer?" yelled Tim. "What did you do to her?"

"Who the hell are you bastards? Get the hell outa my house."

Tim swung his fist into the side of Downy's face. Spit, tears and blood spat from his mouth as his head rolled to the side.

"Gee, I think you hurt him," said Bruce.

"Where the hell is Jennifer?" yelled Tim.

"At the docks…bastards…you're both dead. You don't know who you're fuckin' with."

"What's that? Docks? Talk, damn you!"

"Yeah, up at Beverly."

"Where? Where? She better be alive. You've hurt her and you're dead!"

Bruce sliced his cheek. Downy howled in what must have been considerable pain.

"Where is she!" screamed Tim inches from Downy's face.

"Gateway. In a fuckin' boat," gasped Downy.

Tim went behind Downy. "Keep his hands tied up. We're taking this asshole up to Gateway Marina."

Bruce untangled the cords tying Downy to the chair. "What do we do with him if Jennifer's hurt…or worse."

Tim looked at Bruce for a second. "You walk away…then I'll deal with him."

"You bastards! Who the hell are you? You don't know who you're fuckin' with."

Tim turned to Bruce. "Lets get him in the car and get the hell out of here."

———

Frank Cipriano sat at his desk shaking his head. *Things are coming unfuckin' glued. This is gonna be the end of the road for Downy. I'm done with him.* He picked up his phone and punched in the number for Russo.

"Hello."

"Mario. Quick question. Do you know if that shyster Regis Pearson still owns Gateway Marina out in Beverly? He borrowed a shitload of money from me a couple years ago to reopen that old place. You remember?"

"Yeah…I got it here on my computer. By the way, he still owes you most of it. He's not kept up with the interest. Shit, he's almost a year behind. I should've been keeping an eye on him. I'm sorry."

"Forget about it. I have more pressing things on my mind. You're doing a good job over there at Century. *I'll* put a call in to Regis."

"Thanks, Frank. It's coming together here."

"Good. We'll be talking."

Cipriano looked through his little notebook for the phone number of Regis Pearson and dialed it. The phone rang six times before it was picked up.

"Gateway. Pearson speaking."

"Regis baby, it's your old friend and benefactor, Frank. Remember me? I'm the guy you owe all that money to."

"Hey Frank. Good to hear from you. I…I… I've been having some problems out here. I know I'm way behind. I'll make it up to you…catch up by the end of the year."

Cipriano heard the panic and fear in Regis's voice. "Regis, what am I going to do with you? You're lying to me. I really don't like that. Pisses me off."

"Frank, I…I…"

"Shut up Regis and listen! Are you're hiding that dip-shit Downy up there? Don't lie to me."

"Sure, Frank. He's been up here for a while. Said he didn't want to talk to the FBI. Some crap like that."

"How much he paying you?"

"He gave me five-large. Said there would be more."

"Are you listening to me, Regis?"

"I am, Frank. Yes."

"Did that Downy asshole bring some broad up there, hide her somewhere?"

"He…he said he wouldn't hurt her. Just for a week or so. He swore he wouldn't hurt her."

"You believe him Regis? That five-grand make you a believer?"

"Frank, I…"

"Shut up! Are you listening to me Regis?"

"Yes, Frank."

"Where does that shit-bag have the woman stored?"

"Frank, I…I haven't anything to do with this. He…he…"

"Where?"

"He took her down to an old cabin cruiser that belongs to him. It's tied up at the end of the old pier. He swears she's okay, but I haven't been down there."

"Where is that asshole? Put him on the phone."

"He left a little while ago. Got a call sayin' someone broke into his condo."

"Son of a bitch!…"

Frank punched in another number.

"Hey Frank, what's up."

"Where are you?"

"I'm just leaving Ocean Tower."

"Angelo, things are coming unglued. Our old buddy, Tim what's-his-name, called in a panic. Seems like the Jennifer girl is gone missing. And it seems Downy is missing too. Now, I found out Downy is hiding out in

Gateway Marina, but that Regis dude said he was called away maybe an hour ago; something about a break-in at his condo. Also, Regis tells me Downy has this Jennifer broad stashed away in some dumpy boat he has up there."

"What the hell's going on?"

"I think Downy is trying to figure what to do with the broad so she don't testify. But he doesn't want her dying to come back to him. Maybe going to send her with the fishes. I'm hoping she is still alive. Need you to go up there as fast as you can. You need to get there before Downy gets back or those crazy guys, Tim and Bruce, show up."

"Okay Frank. I'm in my car now. What do I do with Downy when I see him?"

"First we gotta make sure the broad is okay. Then the asshole has to disappear. I'm done with him."

"I'm on it Frank. Call you later."

CHAPTER 28

Special Agent Barrow had obtained a search warrant for the Owens's house, as all attempts at locating Diane had been fruitless. What they really wanted to know was the location of Robert Downy. They were convinced if anyone knew, it would be Diane Owens. Agents Nedham and Barrow stood by their car and looked at the house.

"The place looks abandoned," said Nedham. "Look at all the newspapers at the door."

"Yeah, the yard hasn't been worked on in some time, either. We better see if she's inside."

"If she is, it won't be pretty."

The men walked up to the front door kicking some newspapers out of the way. Agent Barrow knocked many times without getting a response. He then tried the door but it was locked. Nedham went to a window that allowed a view through partially closed blinds into the living room. "This room looks good. Everything's in order."

"Let's check out the rest of the place," said Barrow.

They walked around the house, peering through the windows. Nothing seemed disturbed.

"The yard has really gone to shit," said Nedham.

Agent Barrow went to the back door and examined the door lock; then reached into his pocket for his multi tool.

"Is that a Leatherman?"

"Yep. Let's see if I can get this door open."

"The warrant good for this?" asked Nedham.

"Bet your ass." The door popped open. "We're in."

Nedham flipped the kitchen light switch without effect. "Electric must be off."

"Probably didn't make the payment." Barrow tested another light switch to no avail. "Let's check the rooms, and then we'll look in the garage."

"The place looks abandoned, but it's very neat and clean."

They went into all the rooms to find everything tidy and the beds made up. It appeared as if Diane had just stepped out on an errand. The pile of newspapers had suggested she had been gone for over two weeks.

Barrow pointed to the other side of the kitchen. "That's got to be the door into the garage. Let's take a look."

Nedham tried the light switch. "Not much light in here." He swung his small flashlight to light up the four corners.

"No car. We'll check the airport, but she's probably long gone."

"Let's find her financial papers," suggested Nedham. "See if they tell us anything. I saw a fancy desk in the dining room."

As Nedham pulled out drawers of the desk, they saw that they were empty. In one drawer were several business cards among which Barrow found one for a real estate broker.

He looked at Nedham. "I have to check this out." He pulled out his cell phone and called the number on the card.

"Hello. This is Marlene Augusta at Northeast Prime Properties. How may I help you?"

"Hello, this is FBI Special Agent Walter Barrow. I'm inquiring about a house in Lexington, probably listed by Diane Owens."

"Okay… Yes, I have it here. We haven't prepped it for listing yet. What can I help you with?"

"When was this property put on the market? I didn't see a sign."

"Two weeks ago. Like I said, we haven't got it ready to show yet."

"And that was by Diane Owens?"

"Why yes…"

"Do you have an address for her where the papers will be sent?"

"Not exactly. We *have* been instructed as to how the funds are to be handled in her absence."

"Oh, really? What exactly is the arrangement?"

"We've been given instructions on how to settle funds and papers. Our legal department is taking care of this."

"I'm sure it's all in order, but I'll have one of our investigators come by with a warrant and review the details with you."

"You'll need to contact our legal department. Will there be anything else?"

"You've been a great help. Thank you."

Barrow put the phone back in his pocket, and then turned to Nedham. "Long gone."

Nedham grinned. "She's not coming back."

The two FBI agents went back to their offices in downtown Boston. Barrow looked up as Nedham entered.

"Her car was located in Long Term Parking at Logan. I'm getting it towed this afternoon."

Barrow nodded. "I received a call a few minutes ago. Diane used her passport on entering Mexico City a week ago. Two days later she showed up in Panama City."

"She sure gets around."

"Yeah, well, found out she has personal bank accounts in Mexico City and Panama."

"Any linkage to Century Design or Ocean Tower?"

"No. The accounts are in her name only."

Nedham asked, "Are we talking a lot of money?"

"I'm told they haven't confirmed the account values, but it looks like six figures in each."

"How the heck did she come up with that?"

"That's an interesting question."

"Well, her husband didn't earn that kind of money."

"It turns out Diane and Downy had some joint accounts in Mexican and Panamanian banks. There were some sizeable deposits made over the last two years."

"Wow. The two of them joined at the hip."

"Just prior to her leaving the USA, she transferred fifty percent of these accounts to other accounts that were in her name only."

"This is one smart lady. We have any leverage?"

"The DA's office is looking into it; but at first glance, they don't think so."

"Really?"

"So far… There aren't any criminal charges pending. We don't have any reason at this time to seek her extradition or seize any assets."

"How about local?" asked Nedham.

Barrow shook his head. "Don't know of any. But of course, the main issue is Downy."

"Yeah, like where the hell is he?"

CHAPTER 29

Tim and Bruce got to Gateway Marina with Downy trussed up in the back seat, complaining bitterly of his discomfort. They found the gate closed and no one in sight. Bruce, with a stroke of his knife, forced Downy to tell the key-code to open the gate. They parked at the docks just as another car roared through the still open gate.

They turned to look at the new arrival and recognized Angelo, who waved and yelled for them to wait for him.

"Hey, guys! What are you doing here?"

"We're looking for Jennifer. Downy said she's in that piece-of-shit boat over there." Tim pointed to the decrepit cabin cruiser.

"What? Downy? Where the hell is he?"

"Tied up in the back seat of my car!"

"What? You kiddin' me?" Angelo now stood close to Tim and Bruce. "Where the hell you find him?"

"At his house. We grabbed him. Made him tell us where Jennifer is."

"You gotta be shittin' me! Grabbed him outa his house? He's in your car?"

"Yeah, we're going to search that old boat, see if she's there." Tim started toward the boat "Come on, Bruce."

"Jesus… Yeah, go look." Angelo stood there shaking his head, holding his gun at his side.

Tim and Bruce paused in front of the dilapidated boat. Most of the paint had peeled off and it listed to portside noticeably. They could not see through the grime-clouded windows.

"I'll go in, see if she's there," said Tim.

"I'm going in with you." Bruce jumped onto the deck.

Tim followed immediately. They stood still and listened for any noise from inside. All was quiet. Tim went to the small door at the bridge and yanked it open.

Bruce peered over his shoulder. "See anything?"

"It stinks in here. This is the galley. There's another door beyond."

"Let's go." Bruce gave Tim a shove. "Yank it open."

"Rope holding it closed."

"Yeah. Here, let me cut them."

Tim grabbed the latch and turned it and then yanked the door open. "She's here! My god, she's here!" He saw Jennifer on the floor tied and bound to a support pillar. He knelt alongside her, caressing her face and hair. Tears ran down her face.

Bruce reached behind her head with his pocketknife to cut away the improvised cloth and duct tape gag that had been placed over her mouth. He used the knife to saw through the duct tape and plastic restraints on her wrists and ankles.

She cried and coughed and was incoherent at first. Tim held her and tried to comfort her as she sobbed and trembled. Tears wet Tim's cheek.

Tim turned to Bruce. "Would you get some water and a blanket from the car?"

Bruce stood up. "Yeah. Think she'll be okay?"

"Hope so." He wiped tears away with his fingers.

Bruce turned to leave. "I'll be right back."

Tim rubbed her ankles and wrists, raw from her struggle to get loose. He spoke softly in the hope of calming her near hysteria. Jennifer didn't attempt to get up, just lay her head against Tim's chest and sobbed. When she tried to speak, Tim became aware that she was still terrified, fearful that Downy would be back to kill her. She apologized for her soiled clothes and foul odor; that she hadn't been allowed to go to the bathroom since Downy had brought her here. She wasn't sure how many days it had been.

Bruce returned with a nearly full bottle of water and a car blanket. They let Jennifer drink half of the water, but worried about her getting sick, pulled it away from her. Tim wrapped Jennifer in the blanket and held her against him.

"Think you can stand up?" asked Tim. "We need to get out of here."

When Jennifer tried to stand up she fell. "I…my legs…"

"Bruce, help me get her up. We can't just sit here."

With Tim and Bruce holding her up, Jennifer managed to use her weak legs well enough that they were able to get her outside the cabin and onto the deck. Angelo jumped down onto the deck and helped the two friends struggle to get Jennifer from the shifting boat deck onto the dock.

"Young lady, are you injured?" asked Angelo. "Were you assaulted?"

Jennifer shook her head and hugged the blanket tightly around her shoulders and looked at the ground. Tears ran down her face.

Tim spoke up. "Her ankles and wrists are raw and bleeding from where they tied her. She hasn't had any water or food in days."

"You guys take her up to Seaside General Hospital, just north of here. They'll check her out, she's dehydrated, bad sores. Get moving!"

"In the back of the car," gasped Tim. "*He's* in the car."

"Get going. She needs help," said Angelo, then added. "I'll take care of *him*."

Tim and Bruce looked at each other and nodded. They helped Jennifer walk toward the car.

Angelo ran ahead of them. At the car, he pulled Downy out of the back seat and dragged him toward the office building.

Jennifer was placed in the back seat and Tim wrapped her with the blanket and sat with her. Bruce started the car and headed out of the marina to the next town and the hospital.

"What…what's happening? Was that Downy?" she asked.

Bruce and Tim exchanged glances. Tim pulled her close to him. "He won't bother you anymore."

"Ang, you don't have to do this! We can work it out," Downy pleaded.

"Shut the hell up," said Angelo. "You like beating up young ladies, you bastard?"

"Please! Call him. Let me talk to him. Jesus. Don't do this."

In the office he turned to Regis. "Come outside."

A few steps away from the building, Angelo glared at Regis. "Get one of those twin-engine fast fishing boats and bring it right here." He pointed to a spot along the dock next to a large cabin cruiser. "Tie it up there and wait for me to come out with that lump of shit."

"Jesus, Angelo, what are you going to do? I don't want to be part of anything like that."

"I give a shit what you want? Do what I told you."

Regis hurried off to prepare the fast-boat.

Angelo pulled the phone from his pocket and keyed a number.

"Frank."

"Angelo here. The Jennifer babe is on the way to the hospital with the two dudes."

"What kind of shape she in?"

"Not good. But she'll be okay after a couple days in the hospital. You're not going to believe what I found when I got here."

"What's that?"

"Downy! Fuckin' Downy, tied up in the back of this dude's car…Tim's car. I almost pissed myself."

"No shit? Jesus, those two are full of surprises. Where is that son-of-a-bitch?"

"Regis is getting a fast-boat ready for me."

"I don't want to have to think about that asshole again."

"You won't. He's going deep sea fishing."

"Regis going to be a problem?"

"I doubt it."

CHAPTER 30

Tim and Bruce sat in the waiting room at Seaside General Hospital anxious to be allowed to see Jennifer. The TV was set to the local cable channel with its near continuous news coverage.

"Nothing about Downy," Tim commented.

"Probably better we don't ask," said Bruce.

Just then a nurse announced that Tim and Bruce finally could visit Jennifer. She was taking a saline drip and had just awakened from a sedative. Jennifer smiled when she saw her two friends enter the room.

"You guys are a sight for sore eyes."

"We're sure glad you're okay," offered Tim. "You are, right?"

Jennifer reached for Tim's hand and held it against her chest. "It was dreadful…Downy."

Bruce stood next to Tim. "We didn't know where to look for you. Sorry it took us so long."

"You guys are my heroes. I had almost given up." Tears ran down her cheek. She wiped at them with her free hand. "I was sure he was leaving me there to die."

Tim smiled and squeezed her hand. "Nurse said you could go home tomorrow."

"My clothes…they're all soiled…"

"The nurse said she bagged them and will bring you clean clothes from her daughter's closet. It's really nice of her," said Bruce.

"Yeah. You'll have clean clothes tomorrow," added Tim.

"I'll be so glad to be out of here."

"We'll get you home. You may want to call your parents…let them know you're okay."

"What…what happened to *him*? I…I saw him there."

"Downy? I think Angelo and he went deep sea fishing,"

Jennifer stared from Tim to Bruce. "He…he's…"

"He's with Angelo," said Tim.

"I don't think you'll have to worry about him," said Bruce.

She looked down at her hands. "He was so evil."

"There's probably a grand jury out on Cipriano. And in that case, Downy may have been too big a risk." Tim shrugged, "Just sayin'… Seems like a fitting end considering how his partners disappeared."

"He wouldn't say why he was kidnapping me and hiding me in that old boat. He slapped me when I kept asking. He…he had come to my apartment with a stun gun…he looked crazy…his eyes. He threatened me to keep quiet. I was afraid…if a cop stopped us…what he would do."

"Jesus, I even called Cipriano and asked for his help to find you," said Tim.

"What…what did he say?"

"He kept saying he would get back to me. I didn't hear back. I wonder if Angelo…"

"Maybe he did help us," said Jennifer.

"It had to have been him," said Bruce.

CHAPTER 31

Tim and Bruce went to the hospital the next morning after Jennifer called Tim to tell him she was ready to be discharged. She held onto Tim's arm as they left the wheelchair behind at the curb to get into the car. She didn't let go of him until she was eased into a seat. She asked many questions of Tim and Bruce as Tim drove toward Lowell and Jennifer's apartment. But there were periods of quiet where Jennifer seemed to want to be alone with her thoughts. Tim first stopped the car in front of Bruce's apartment building. Bruce got out, said he'd call the next day. Jennifer thanked him again for helping to find her.

It was a slow walk from the car to Jennifer's apartment. Tim heard her sob a few times before they entered her unit. Inside the door, Tim held her as she cried for a few minutes. Then she declared she had to take a long hot shower and put on her own clothes. She asked Tim to toss the clothes from the nurse into the washing machine; she wanted to return them.

Tim heard the shower come on as he gathered up her clothes. He went to the laundry alcove and tossed them into the washing machine. As the machine started filling, he stood there and wondered what he could do to help her.

Jennifer came out of her bedroom dressed in jeans and a sweatshirt. Her hair was done up in a ponytail.

"You look nice."

She came to him and wrapped her arms around his waist and hugged him. "Thanks for helping me…and for being here. I don't say this very often, but I do love you."

Tim kissed her wet cheeks. "I love you, too."

"I want to go to my parent's place. Okay?"

Tim nodded. "I can follow you there. That way you have your car."

"Okay. I'll pack some things."

Tim made coffee while Jennifer put away her clothes. The phone rang and Tim grabbed it from the wall hoping to get it before Jennifer picked it up. "I got it," he called loudly.

"Hello."

"This is Roy Wilson. May I speak to her?"

"Just a moment. I'll check."

Tim went to Jennifer's bedroom and knocked on the partially open door. "Jen, it's your Uncle Roy. He'd like to speak to you."

"Okay. I'll be right out."

Jennifer took the phone from Tim. "Uncle Roy?"

"I'm so glad to hear your voice. What a dreadful experience that had to have been. How are you feeling now?"

"I'm starting to feel human again. I owe so much to Tim and Bruce."

"Seems like your nemesis came to a bad end."

"Sad, the way it happened. But he was evil."

"I think you should be prepared to address any upcoming legal issues or court cases. The FBI will be investigating all that's happened. I'm sure of it. I can have a good attorney get in touch with you. He'll treat you well."

"Okay. I'll work with him."

"Jennifer, your parents are worried sick. Please call them and put their minds at ease."

"I will. Thanks for calling."

Jennifer handed the phone to Tim who hung it back on the kitchen wall. "I'll call my parents from my bedroom; it could get involved."

"Okay. I'll watch the TV news."

She kissed him and went into her bedroom.

Jennifer just completed a call to her parents vacationing in Italy. As she stepped out of her bedroom, the phone rang again. She motioned for Tim to stay seated and took the call in the kitchen.

"Hello."

"Jennifer, this is Frank Cipriano. I'm glad you got free of that deplorable situation, and I hope you are recovering well."

"I…I am. I appreciate whatever help you gave my friends. I thank you for that."

"Hey, thank your two friends. They're a real pain in the ass but they did the job."

"Yes, I owe them and you a lot."

"Jennifer, I wanted to ask if you and your friends could avoid saying much to the press beyond the obvious, since Mr. Russo and I are preparing to defend Century Design to the SEC."

"Okay. I'll mention it to them. I don't think there'll be a problem."

"I'm trying to keep Century in one piece."

"I understand. Thanks again for the help you gave us."

"Forget about it."

"'Bye."

The following day Tim and Jennifer met Bruce at a pizza shop in Chelmsford to discuss current circumstances and plans they had for the future. A corner booth offered them a quiet place without fear of being overheard.

"So, Tim, I'm keeping my lawyer on retainer for the next few months," said Bruce. "Things still look a little shaky to me what with the different investigations that are going on. I think I'll be called as a witness on some of this." Bruce looked at his friends. "You guys could be called as witnesses and probably will be. My lawyer could help you if it came to that."

Tim nodded. "Thanks. I think you're right."

"I'm still nervous and afraid," said Jennifer. "I know Downy is dead. I know. But I can't help it."

"It's sure understandable," said Bruce. "Jesus, Jennifer, it was terrible what Downy put you through."

"I'm going to stay with Jennifer at her parent's condo, said Tim, "for a while at least."

"I'll be looking for a job," said Jennifer. "Tim and I are going to stay together." She squeezed Tim's arm.

"Yeah, you two are an item; always knew that," said Bruce. "By the way, I talked with Frank Cipriano. Actually, he called me. We clarified what I can reveal in an upcoming article about the Century Design debacle. He wants me to only tell of the main public issues and events, and not to go into any depth."

"That's tying you up pretty well, isn't it?" asked Tim.

"Yeah, I'll have to deal with it. Cipriano said he and Russo are preparing to defend the Century Design model in front of the SEC and doesn't want additional problems. He wants any article I write about this to be approved by him, Russo, or his lawyer. Also, he said the FBI was inquiring into Century Design business dealings and some charges may result."

"What are the real issues with the Century business model that has the SEC worked up?" asked Tim.

"Well, as I understand it, it is the commingling of investor funds as part of the investment strategy that gives the investment fund greater leverage in the negotiation of fees where funds are invested and reduces the cost of fund administration."

"Complicated," said Tim. "What's the law say about it?"

"The law says commingling is a breach of trust in which a fiduciary mixes funds held in care for a client with their own funds. It makes it difficult to determine which funds belong to the fiduciary and which belong to the client." Bruce smiled. "In the case of Century, one could say that was the whole idea. We'll let that pass for now."

"Interesting approach," Tim commented.

"This raises particular concerns where the funds are invested, and gains or losses from the investments must be allocated. In such circumstances, the law usually presumes that any gains run to the client and any losses run to the fiduciary that is guilty of commingling."

"Who gives a shit? I'm getting a head ache," said Tim.

"Me too," said Jennifer.

Bruce grinned. "Well, okay. There are a zillion rules having to do with investment and bankruptcy regarding commingled funds, but we don't need to get into it all. Leave that to Russo."

"Say Bruce, what do you know of Diane Owens?" asked Jennifer.

"I can't get a clear story on her. The FBI ain't talking about any of this. I guess the FBI is trying to link together all that happened."

"So, what about Diane Owens?" insisted Jennifer.

"I called all my sources. It appears she has the last laugh. Last I heard, a reporter friend at the Globe said that Downy was responsible for the death of her husband, according to Massachusetts State Police sources. So far I haven't heard where authorities could establish any link from Diane to her husband's murder or the elimination of Downy."

"So that's it? She's free?" said Jennifer.

Bruce nodded. "She gave us all the last laugh."

"So, what's happening now?" asked Tim.

"I heard the court agreed to put Russo as temporary head of Century Design as petitioned by Cipriano. I imagine the DOJ will be requesting a grand jury investigation of Century and Cipriano's role in it."

Jennifer shook her head. "So, she's free as a bird with a bunch of Downy's money."

Tim nodded, "One smart lady."